Knowledge Management

M000309944

The discipline of knowledge management (KM) is rapidly becoming established as an essential course or module in both information systems and management programs around the world. Many KM texts pitch theoretical issues at too technical or high a level, or present only a theoretical prescriptive treatment of knowledge or KM modeling "problems." The *Knowledge Management Primer* provides students with an essential understanding of KM approaches by examining the purpose and nature of its key components. The book demystifies the KM field by explaining in a precise, accessible manner the key concepts of KM tools, strategies and techniques, and their benefits to contemporary organizations. Readers will find this book filled with approaches to managing and developing KM that are underpinned by theory and research, are integrative in nature, and address "softer" approaches in manifesting and recognizing knowledge.

Rajeev K. Bali is a Reader in Healthcare Knowledge Management at Coventry University. He heads the Knowledge Management for Healthcare (KARMAH) research subgroup (part of the Biomedical Computing and Engineering Technologies (BIOCORE) Applied Research Group) based in the Health Design and Technology Institute (HDTI).

Nilmini Wickramasinghe is Associate Professor at the Stuart School of Business, Illinois Institute of Technology, and Co-director of the IIT Center for the Management of Medical Technology, Chicago, U.S.

Brian Lehaney is Professor of Systems Management in Coventry University's Faculty of Engineering and Computing.

Routledge Series in Information Systems

Edited by Steve Clarke (Hull University Business School, U.K.),
M. Adam Mahmood (University of Texas at El Paso, U.S.), and
Morten Thanning Vendelø (Copenhagen Business School, Denmark)

The overall aim of the series is to provide a range of textbooks for advanced undergraduate and postgraduate study and to satisfy the advanced undergraduate and postgraduate markets, with a focus on key areas of those curricula.

The key to success lies in delivering the correct balance between organizational, managerial, technological, theoretical and practical aspects. In particular, the interaction between, and inter-dependence of, these often different perspectives is an important theme. All texts demonstrate a "theory into practice" perspective, whereby the relevant theory is discussed only in so far as it contributes to the applied nature of the domain. The objective here is to offer a balanced approach to theory and practice.

Information Systems is a rapidly developing and changing domain, and any book series needs to reflect current developments. It is also a global domain, and a specific aim of this series, as reflected in the international composition of the editorial team, is to reflect its global nature. The purpose is to combine state-of-the-art topics with global perspectives.

Information Systems Strategic Management 2nd edition

An Integrated Approach
Steve Clarke

Managing Information and Knowledge in Organizations: A Literacy Approach

Alistair Mutch

Knowledge Management Primer

Rajeev K. Bali, Nilmini Wickramasinghe, Brian Lehaney

Healthcare Knowledge Management Primer

Nilmini Wickramasinghe, Rajeev K. Bali, Brian Lehaney, Jonathan L. Schaffer, M. Chris Gibbons

Knowledge Management Primer

Rajeev K. Bali
Nilmini Wickramasinghe
Brian Lehaney

Routledge
Taylor & Francis Group

NEW YORK AND LONDON

First published 2009
by Routledge
270 Madison Ave, New York, NY 10016

Simultaneously published in the U.K.
by Routledge
2 Park Square, Milton Park, Abingdon, Oxon OX14 4RN

Routledge is an imprint of the Taylor & Francis Group, an informa business

© 2009 Rajeev K. Bali, Nilmini Wickramasinghe, Brian Lehaney

Typeset in Perpetua and Bell Gothic by
Florence Production Ltd., Stoodleigh, Devon

All rights reserved. No part of this book may be reprinted or reproduced or
utilised in any form or by any electronic, mechanical, or other means, now
known or hereafter invented, including photocopying and recording, or in
any information storage or retrieval system, without permission in writing
from the publishers.

Trademark Notice: Product or corporate names may be trademarks or
registered trademarks, and are used only for identification and explanation
without intent to infringe.

Library of Congress Cataloging in Publication Data
Knowledge Management Primer/Rajeev K. Bali,
    Nilmini Wickramasinghe, Brian Lehaney.
        p. cm.——(Routledge series in information systems)
    Includes bibliographical references and index.
    1. Knowledge management.   2. Management information systems.
    I. Wickramasinghe, Nilmini.   II. Lehaney, Brian, 1953–.   III. Title.
    [DNLM: 1. Medical Informatics.   2. Information Management.]
    HD30.2.B353 2009
    658.4'038—dc22   2008047984

ISBN10: 0–415–99232–X (hbk)
ISBN10: 0–415–99233–8 (pbk)
ISBN10: 0–203–89471–5 (ebk)

ISBN13: 978–0–415–99232–9 (hbk)
ISBN13: 978–0–415–99233–6 (pbk)
ISBN13: 978–0–203–89471–2 (ebk)

For our families and friends

BERNARD WOOLLEY:
"But you only need to know things on a need to know basis."

SIR HUMPHREY APPLEBY:
"I need to know everything! How else can I judge
whether or not I need to know it?"

Yes, Prime Minister, (Man Overboard),
written by Jonathan Lynn and Sir Antony Jay

Contents

Figures

Tables

Preface

"The basic economic resource——the means of production——is no longer capital, nor natural resources, nor labor. It is and will be knowledge."

Peter Drucker

THE REASON FOR THIS BOOK

Knowledge Management (KM) is an approach that is very much in vogue, despite immense confusion over its contents and efficacy. Many managers (and indeed academics) remain skeptical over its numerous merits despite not fully understanding the field.

The motivation for this book was simple——to produce a text that introduces the multi-faceted aspects of contemporary KM in a simple way. This book aims to explore the area of KM from the "bottom up" in order to facilitate and/or reinforce understanding of key concepts. We believe that there are numerous KM texts, which either deal with the subject at too high a level——thus skirting over first principles——or are so tangential to the subject as to be irrelevant. The plethora of books currently available on the subject largely fail to do this and assume an in-depth understanding of KM before describing potential and actual applications.

This book therefore deals with the very essence of KM and describes component parts in a simple and easy to understand manner. The three essential components of KM (namely people, process and technology) are presented and explored in a clear manner.

Our combined extensive experience in both the academic and business worlds allows us to discuss concepts that are both academically-grounded and credible, while remaining vocationally relevant and applicable.

AIMS OF THE BOOK

The general aim of the book is to provide a theoretically and empirically grounded approach to KM. The discipline of KM is rapidly becoming established as an essential course or module in the Higher Education sector around the world. Such courses and modules may be at either undergraduate or postgraduate level. Research students, perhaps with no formal KM training, require essential skills in order to pursue their studies. Similarly, managers at all levels in industry and commerce often find the KM subject area to be both intriguing and confusing.

This book will explore and explain the nature of essential KM components skills in an introductory and easy to understand way. Accessibility and usability in this manner would be of use to both novice and amateur students and professionals wishing to learn more about the KM field.

The book would provide readers with an understanding of approaches to KM by examining the purpose and nature of its key components. The rationale of the text is to demystify the KM field by explaining in an accessible manner the key concepts of KM tools, strategies and techniques, and their benefits to contemporary organizations.

The text will demonstrate how, with practice and understanding, students can apply its key precepts. Generally, each chapter is followed by a suitable case exercise (with questions), from which readers can apply the key principles from the chapter.

WHO SHOULD USE THIS BOOK?

The book is targeted at students and novice practitioners new to the area of KM. As mentioned, KM has evolved from existing disciplines such as organizational behavior, ICT and human factors—some understanding and appreciation of these areas would be beneficial. The main academic audience is MBA (Master of Business Administration) students, but it is also aimed at supporting final year undergraduate studies in, for example, business studies and information science, post-experience courses (e.g. NVQ (National Vocational Qualification), DMS (Diploma in Management Studies)), and other Masters courses (information management (IM), and other courses where IM forms a key part). For MBA, this is a core subject, while for undergraduate, other post-experience, and other Masters courses, it is more likely to be a supporting text. The main vocational audience would include managers and practitioners working in the information management fields wanting to learn more about how KM could bring about organizational benefits.

STRUCTURE AND DISTINCTIVE FEATURES OF THE BOOK

The layout followed is standard for the Routledge Information Systems Series. The aim of this, together with the supplied instructor's manual, is to provide a basis for courses of academic study at the levels identified within its target audience:

- Case examples are provided.
- Each chapter concludes with a Review and Discussion questions.
- Case exercises are provided for each chapter.
- Further reading is suggested at the end of each chapter.

Issues in KM are fully integrated with current thinking in organizational theory; in particular, we focus on design or planning aspects as well as the more human-centric and participative approaches (which in themselves are very similar to the IS "soft" or human-centered methods). This book aims to do justice to all strategic developments seen to be of relevance to the KM arena, ranging from the planned and political to the totally participative and emancipatory. To achieve this, key approaches to KM are addressed and related to organizations, allowing the emergence of a synthesized approach to KM strategy, which is firmly grounded on current thinking.

USE OF THE BOOK FOR TEACHING

In terms of specific pedagogical features:

- Each chapter begins with learning objectives. Chapters are summarized, and key words and phrases listed. Questions for review and questions for discussion are given towards the end of each chapter.
- Suggested further reading, with a guide as to the relevance of the reading suggested, and references appear at the end of each chapter.
- Case exercises and questions to be addressed by the cases are given. Generally the plan is to provide one per chapter, but some chapters may not lend themselves to the use of case material.
- A glossary is provided at the end of the book.

A full instructor's guide is provided on the World Wide Web.

- An instructor's manual is provided containing study guides (with lecture plans and overhead transparencies), worked examples, answers to review questions and discussion questions, and suggested approaches to case studies. The instructor's manual also gives suggested assignment questions not given in the main text.
- Suggested schemes of work are provided.
- The instructor's guide is split into the same chapters as the book, and for each chapter:

  - a lecture plan is given;
  - key issues are identified for the lectures, together with overhead projector slides;
  - answers to review questions, discussion questions and case exercises are provided; and
  - suggestions for assignments are given.

Rajeev K. Bali
Knowledge Management for Healthcare
(KARMAH) Research Subgroup
Biomedical Computing and
Engineering Technologies (BIOCORE)
Applied Research Group
Health Design and Technology Institute (HDTI)
Coventry University
COVENTRY
U.K.
r.bali@ieee.org

Nilmini Wickramasinghe
Center for the Management of
Medical Technology (CMMT)
Stuart School of Business
Illinois Institute of Technology
CHICAGO
U.S.
nilmini@stuart.iit.edu

Brian Lehaney
Department of Engineering and
Knowledge Management
Coventry University
COVENTRY
U.K.
b.lehaney@coventry.ac.uk

August 2008

Acknowledgements

Many thanks to Prof. Steve Clarke (Series Editor) for green-lighting the project and for his insightful comments and support during the project period. Particular thanks are reserved for Nancy Hale (Editor) and Felisa Salvago-Keyes (Editorial Assistant) at Routledge in New York for their support and enthusiasm, as well as all the other members of the Routledge editorial team for their invaluable assistance in helping this book to take shape.

We thank the following graduate students for their contributions in the form of case studies: Manuel Gayle, Kevin Grisez, Monica Louie, Daniel Milosevic, Richard Morrow, Devaraj Ramsamy, Vernell Robinson, David Rogers, Siobhan Sudberry, Shad Sungren and Daren Thompson.

We acknowledge our respective universities for affording us the time to work on this project as well as our numerous friends and colleagues for their varied and stimulating discussions and interactions; the "social network" aspect of KM was indeed in force.

Many of the schematics included in this text were very kindly supplied to us by *Doctrina Applied Research and Consulting LLC* (www.consultdoctrina.com) and we are grateful to all involved for their excellent contributions.

We thank Prof. Jay Liebowitz (Carey Business School, Johns Hopkins University, U.S.) for writing such a fine foreword and for his insights into the world of KM.

We reserve special thanks to Jonathan Lynn and Sir Antony Jay for their kind permission to reproduce lines from *Yes, Prime Minister* (from the chapter/episode entitled *Man Overboard*).

Foreword

"Knowledge Management (KM)" is a term that has been applied over the past fifteen years, yet surprisingly, many organizations still haven't woven KM principles, concepts, techniques and applications into their organizational fabric. KM deals with how best to leverage knowledge internally and externally, and today's organizations need to apply these concepts in order to be competitive in today's and tomorrow's marketplace.

This new *Knowledge Management Primer* book by Bali, Wickramasinghe and Lehaney provides a quick guide for organizations to better understand the fundamentals and merits of KM. Case studies are sprinkled throughout the book, providing the reinforcement to see how organizations are applying these concepts. The authors have many years of experience in the KM field, and they give keen insight about the KM world.

In today's environment, the use of KM approaches, including social networking, data mining, lessons learned systems, communities of practice, organizational narratives, expertise locator systems, and the like, is important for organizations to stimulate creativity, build their institutional memory, organize corporate knowledge and develop a strong sense of community in the workplace. Knowledge retention and human capital strategy play a key role in KM as the workforce is becoming grayer and the Baby Boomers are nearing retirement.

Finding ways to capture, share and leverage this knowledge before it is lost are important activities for the thriving livelihood of organizations. By identifying, capturing, sharing and applying knowledge, the hope is that new knowledge is created in the form of products and services to further stimulate innovation. Cross-generational knowledge flows become important in organizations as well to ensure that the transfer of knowledge is occurring between generations. Mentoring, onboarding, job rotation and other personalization approaches to KM should be incorporated into the organization's KM strategy.

KM is a wonderful field that takes advantage of a multidisciplinary approach from organizational behavior, information technology (IT), sociology, cognitive psychology, human resources management, library sciences and other related fields. Certainly, we are seeing a number of universities offering courses and degree programs in KM, and there are KM certification programs being offered throughout industry. We need to continue to educate the "workforce of the future" on how best to utilize these KM techniques, which have been proven to provide direct benefit to the organization's bottom line.

This book serves the above role: to better educate tomorrow's leaders about the value of KM. This Primer allows a quick introduction into KM and provides food for thought to stimulate one's neurons for determining ways to further advance the organization's strategies and goals. Even if you pick and then apply just one or two gems of wisdom from each chapter, your organization should benefit in some way. The book is filled with knowledge nuggets, so sit back and enjoy the reading as you further prepare for your KM journey.

Jay Liebowitz, D.Sc.
Professor, Carey Business School
Johns Hopkins University
Jliebow1@jhu.edu
August 2008

Chapter 1

What is Knowledge Management?

INTRODUCTION

Knowledge Management (KM) is a key approach designed to aid superior decision making and solve current business problems such as competitiveness and the need to innovate in a dynamic, complex and global environment (Wickramasinghe and von Lubitz, 2007). The premise for the need for KM is based on a paradigm shift in the business environment where knowledge is now recognized as central to organizational performance (Drucker, 1993; Ichijo and Nonaka, 2007; Jafari *et al.*, 2008). This macro-level paradigm shift also has significant implications upon the micro-level processes of assimilation and implementation of KM concepts and techniques (Swan *et al.*, 1999), i.e. the Knowledge Management Systems (KMS) that are in place.

We are not only in a new millennium but also a new era. A variety of terms, such as the Post-Industrial Era (Huber, 1990), the Information Age (Shapario and Verian, 1999), the Third Wave (Hope and Hope, 1997) or the Knowledge Society (Drucker, 1999), have been used to describe this epoch. Whichever term is used, there is agreement that one of the key defining and unifying themes of this period is KM. However, nearly ten years into this new millennium still too many practitioners and researchers alike, not to mention students, struggle to understand "what is KM?"

Given the importance of KM to all business operations, irrespective of industry or geographical location, understanding KM has become an imperative for researchers and practitioners. This book is intended to dispel any myths and help the reader understand what KM is and what it is not.

KNOWLEDGE MANAGEMENT (KM)

Central to KM is organizational knowledge, which exists at the confluence of people, process and technology (see Figure 1.1).

The key objective of KM is to create value from an organization's intangible, as well as tangible, assets (Wigg, 1993). It is partly an amalgamation of concepts borrowed from numerous bodies of literature, including: artificial intelligence/knowledge-based systems, software

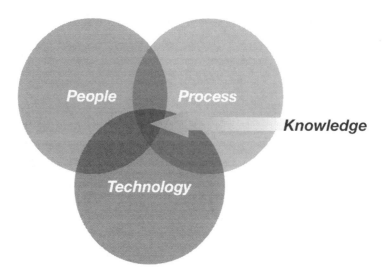

Figure 1.1 *Knowledge: Intersection of People, Process and Technology.*
Reproduced with kind permission of Doctrina Applied Research and Consulting LLC — www.consultdoctrina.com

engineering, BPR (business process re-engineering), human resources, data mining management and organizational behavior (Liebowitz, 1999). However, it is important to note that while KM might have developed from the confluence of these numerous bodies of literature, KM itself is not BPR or data mining, and KM offers something new.

In essence then, KM not only involves the production of information but also the capture of data at the source, the transmission and analysis of this data, as well as the communication of information based on or derived from the data to those who can act on it (Davenport and Prusak, 1998). Moreover, unlike data management which typically focuses on organizing and refining data as a means to an end, or information management that is predominately concerned with structuring and categorizing information, integral to KM is the extraction of relevant data, pertinent information and germane knowledge to aid in superior decision making (Wickramasinghe and von Lubitz, 2007). The relevance of the data, the pertinence of the information and the germaneness of the knowledge are determined by the specific context.

HOW DID KNOWLEDGE MANAGEMENT COME ABOUT?

There are few who would argue that the current business environment is global as well as complex and dynamic. To survive in such an environment requires the attainment of a competitive advantage. Such a competitive advantage must be sustainable, i.e. difficult for competitors to imitate.

Sustainable competitive advantage is dependent on building and exploiting an organization's core competencies (Prahalad and Hamel, 1990). In order to sustain competitive advantage, resources that are idiosyncratic (and thus scarce), and hence difficult to transfer or replicate, are of paramount importance (Grant, 1991). A knowledge-based view of the firm identifies knowledge as the organizational asset that enables sustainable competitive advantage, especially in hyper competitive environments (Davenport and Prusak, 1998; Alavi, 1999; Zack, 1999). This is attributed to the fact that barriers exist regarding the transfer and replication of knowledge (Alavi, 1999); thus making knowledge and KM of strategic significance (Kanter, 1999).

Since the late 1980s, organizations have embraced technology at an exponential rate. This rapid rate of adoption and diffusion of ICTs (information and communication technologies), coupled with the ever increasing data stored in databases or information that is being continually exchanged throughout networks, necessitates organizations to develop and embrace appropriate tools, tactics, techniques and technologies to facilitate prudent management of these raw knowledge assets; i.e. adopt KM.

Finally, during the late 1990s many organizations, especially in the U.S., have been experiencing significant downsizing and the reduction of senior employees. These employees over time have gained much experience and expertise and, as they leave their respective organizations, this expertise leaves too. In an attempt to stem the loss of expertise and vital know-how, organizations needed to embrace KM.

Taking together the need for a sustainable competitive advantage, the need to manage terabytes of data and information, and the need to retain vital expertise and knowledge residing in experts' heads, organizations throughout the world are turning to KM solutions.

KEY CONCEPTS

In order to understand what KM is, it is essential to understand several key concepts. Since, KM addresses the generation, representation, storage, transfer and transformation of knowledge (Hedlund, 1990), the knowledge architecture is designed to capture knowledge and thereby enable KM processes to take place. Underlying the knowledge architecture is the recognition of the binary nature of knowledge; namely its objective and subjective components. Knowledge can exist as an object, in essentially two forms, explicit or factual knowledge, which is typically written or documented knowledge, and tacit or "know how," which typically resides in people's heads (Polanyi, 1958, 1966).

It is well established that while both types of knowledge are important, tacit knowledge, as it is intangible, is more difficult to identify and thus manage (Nonaka, 1991, 1994). Further, objective knowledge, be it tacit or explicit, can be located at various levels; e.g. the individual, group or organization (Hedlund, 1990). Of equal importance, though perhaps less well defined, knowledge also has a subjective component and can be viewed as an ongoing phenomenon, being shaped by social practices of communities (Boland and Tenkasi, 1995).

The objective elements of knowledge can be thought of as primarily having an impact on process. Underpinning such a perspective is a Lockean/Leibnitzian standpoint (Malhotra, 2000; Wickramasinghe and von Lubitz, 2007) where knowledge leads to greater effectiveness and efficiency. In contrast, the subjective elements of knowledge typically impact innovation by supporting divergent or multiple meanings consistent with Hegelian/Kantian modes of inquiry (ibid.) essential for brainstorming or idea generation and social discourse. Both effective and efficient processes, as well as the function of supporting and fostering innovation, are key concerns of KM in theory. These issues are critical if a sustainable competitive advantage is to be attained as well as maximization of an organization's tangible and intangible assets.

The knowledge architecture recognizes these two different, yet key aspects of knowledge and provides the blueprints for an all-encompassing KMS (Wickramasinghe and von Lubitz, 2007). By so doing, the knowledge architecture is defining a KMS that supports both objective and subjective attributes of knowledge. The pivotal function underlined by the knowledge architecture is the flow of knowledge. The flow of knowledge is fundamentally enabled (or not) by the KMS.

In addition, it is possible to change from one type of knowledge to another type of knowledge and this too must be captured in the knowledge architecture. Specifically, as proposed by Nonaka (1994), there exist four possible transformations: 1) combination—where new explicit knowledge is created from existing bodies of explicit knowledge, 2) externalization—where new explicit knowledge is created from tacit knowledge, 3) internalization—where new tacit knowledge is created from explicit knowledge, and 4) socialization—where new tacit knowledge is created from existing tacit knowledge. The continuous change and enriching process of the extant knowledge base is known as the knowledge spiral (Nonaka, 1994).

Once the knowledge architecture has been developed, it is then necessary to consider the knowledge infrastructure. The knowledge infrastructure consists of technology components and people that together make up the knowledge sharing system, and hence it is a socio-technical system (Wickramasinghe and von Lubitz, 2007). Table 1.1 provides a succinct definition of these key concepts relating to KM.

Table 1.1 *Key KM Concepts*

Concept	Definition
Tacit knowledge	Knowledge that resides in peoples' heads , "know how"
Explicit knowledge	Knowledge that is written down as facts, "know what"
Knowledge architecture	The blueprints for identifying where subjective and objective knowledge and /or tacit and explicit knowledge reside in an organization
Knowledge infrastructure	The design of the socio-technical requirements for ensuring appropriate KM, i.e. the design of the necessary people and technology requirements for facilitating KM in a specific organization
Objective perspective of knowledge	Following the Lokean/Leibnitzian forms of inquiry, such knowledge facilitates greater effectiveness and efficiency
Subjective perspective of knowledge	Following the Hegalian/Kantian schools of inquiry, such knowledge facilitates sense making and innovation
Knowledge spiral	The transformation of one type of knowledge to another
Socialization	The transformation of tacit knowledge into new tacit knowledge
Internalization	The transformation of explicit knowledge into new tacit knowledge
Externalization	The transformation of tacit knowledge into new explicit knowledge
Combination	The transformation of explicit knowledge into new explicit knowledge

DATA, INFORMATION, KNOWLEDGE AND WISDOM

Data is a series of discrete events, observations, measurements or facts that can take the form of numbers, words, sounds and/or images. Most useful organizational data is in the form of transaction records, stored in databases and generated through various business processes and activities. Today organizations generate large amounts of multi-spectral data. Given its discrete form, data in itself may not be very useful and thus it is often termed a raw knowledge asset. When data is processed, and organized into a context, it becomes information.

Information is data that has been arranged into a meaningful pattern and thus has a recognizable shape; i.e. data that has been endowed with relevance and purpose. An example is a report created from intelligent database queries. ICTs (information and communication technology) not only enhance the communication capabilities with data but also facilitate the transferring and processing of this data into information.

According to Webster's Dictionary, knowledge is the fact or condition of knowing something with familiarity gained through experience or association. Another useful way to understand knowledge is to define it as contextualized information. The literature is peppered with numerous definitions of knowledge. However, a frequently referenced definition is that given by Davenport and Prusak (1998: 5):

- Knowledge is a fluid mix of framed experiences, values, contextual information, and expert insights that provides a framework for evaluating and incorporating new experiences and information. It originates and is applied in the minds of knowers. In organizations, it is often embedded not only in documents or repositories but also in organizational routine, processes, practices and norms.

It is important to note that this definition is both broad and recognizes that knowledge is indeed not a homogenous construct. It is widely agreed that beyond knowledge lies wisdom (Wickramasinghe and von Lubitz, 2007). Wisdom is essentially a process by which we are able to discern, or judge, between right and wrong, good and bad. In essence, it embodies more of an understanding of fundamental principles embodied within the knowledge that are essentially the basis for the knowledge being what it is.

What is particularly interesting to researchers is the transformation from data to information to knowledge and even wisdom. Figure 1.2 depicts the generally accepted relationship between data, information, knowledge and wisdom.

However, several researchers have suggested other ideas, among them Snowden's (2005) notion that the effective transition to knowledge should also include an element of sense-making (i.e. how can we make sense of the world so we can act in it?). Sense-making is associated with the work of Weick (1995) and Dervin (1998). Figure 1.3 shows how sense-making can be integrated into the "move" towards knowledge.

The conventional (or traditionally accepted) view of data, information and knowledge (a suitable example of which is Figure 1.2) suggests that there is a hierarchical relationship between these items. Other schematics depict this linkage as a pyramid (with wisdom taking pride of place at the top). This can be confusing if one accepts that one is automatically "better" or more useful than the item underneath. Making sense of information (via sense-making as in Figure 1.3) can be of great assistance.

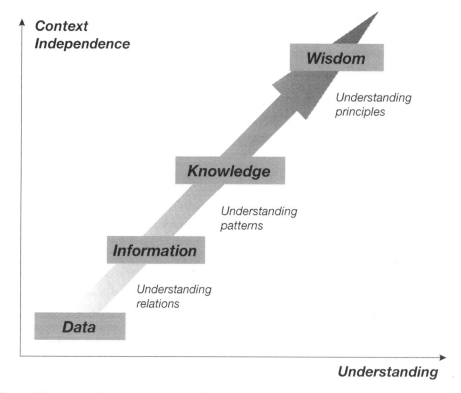

Figure 1.2 *The "Traditional" View of Data-Information-Knowledge-Wisdom.*

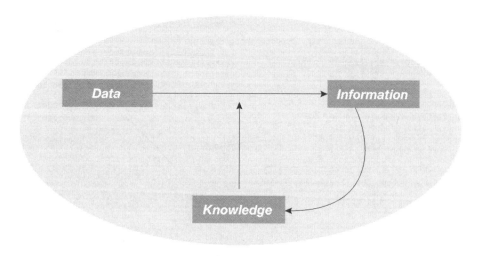

Figure 1.3 *Sense-making and Knowledge*

Source: Snowden (2005)

CONCLUSIONS

This chapter has set out to define what KM is, and explain how and why organizations need KM if they are to be successful. The chapter has also presented several key concepts that are essential to know in order to begin to have a thorough understanding of KM. These include explicit and tacit knowledge, objective and subjective perspectives, the knowledge spiral (and its four key knowledge transformations), knowledge architecture and knowledge infrastructure. In addition, the chapter has presented the terms data, information and wisdom, and has explained how knowledge is different from each of these and yet how it is also connected.

On completion of this chapter the reader should be able to define clearly and succinctly what KM is and what it is not.

SUMMARY

- KM is not just project management.
- KM is not just a fad.
- KM is not just data mining.
- KM is not BPR.
- KM is comprised of a set of tools, techniques, tactics and technologies aimed at maximizing an organization's intangible assets through the extraction of relevant data, pertinent information and germane knowledge, to facilitate superior decision making so that an organization attains and maintains sustainable competitive advantage.

REVIEW QUESTIONS

1 What is KM?
2 Why is KM necessary for current businesses?
3 What is the knowledge spiral and four transformations of knowledge?
4 What is a sustainable competitive advantage?
5 What are the myths of KM?

DISCUSSION QUESTIONS

1 Do you think tacit knowledge or explicit knowledge is more important for an organization and why?

2 Do you think the need for a sustainable competitive advantage, the need to manage terabytes of data and information or the need to retain key organizational expertise played the most important part in the development and embracing of KM by organizations?

CASE EXERCISE: CHICAGO MERCANTILE EXCHANGE (CME GROUP)[1]

Introduction

The CME Group is on the cutting edge of technology, employing numerous information systems to facilitate its operations. Such information systems govern the front, middle and back office functions of the CME Group and are critical in the competitive environment in which it operates. Front office functionality supports trading and order management, the bulk of CME's business functions, while the middle and back office support the functions of the front office.

The latter offices ensure trades are recorded and accounted for, and also ensure that the guidelines for regulatory compliance are met. The co-ordination and operation of these systems is not only of the utmost importance to CME itself but to the market as a whole, as it provides risk management, liquidity and confidence to its stakeholders.

Business Objectives of the Firm

CME's primary business functions are to be an innovative market leader in the derivatives industry and to set the global benchmark in its performance and product offerings. By being the leader, it needs to employ the latest technology and processes in this rapidly changing market environment. Without pushing the envelope and constantly innovating, CME loses its edge to others in the global markets. CME provides a range of products from FX, Interest Rate, Futures and Options. It consistently delivers these products and services by setting the global standard and being an active participant in its industry and influencing those stakeholders in other industries, such as technology. Technology has not only been the backbone of CME's success but also holds the future for the company for years to come.

Industry Analysis

A useful method to provide an objective industry analysis can be achieved using Porter's well known Competitive Analysis (or Five Forces) Model:

■ *Bargaining power of customers*—the high volume of trading that CME experiences gives it a lot more power over customers than a small company would have. If you want to trade derivatives then this is the place to go. They have this advantage due to their size and because of the presence of substitute inputs. As regarded customers, large investment firms would have much more power due to the dollar value that they bring to the floor, but their power is still limited. The bargaining power of customers is weak, as the exchange is the only place in the world to trade certain derivatives. Additionally, the exchange has a high degree of liquidity, making it the prime place to trade derivatives.

■ *Bargaining power of suppliers*—suppliers of technology equipment and services are catering to the needs of the exchange. The demands from the volume of data are pushing the limits of the technological envelope and placing demands on the suppliers of technology to produce the best equipment. The financial industry is now becoming one of the largest consumers of technology, thus making it a prime customer for their suppliers. The bargaining power of suppliers is weak in this industry.

■ *Threat of new entrants*—due to the worldwide infrastructure needed to operate a global firm effectively, it is very difficult to enter this industry. This is just one of the many barriers to entry facing new entrants. Brand equity is paramount in this industry because customers must trust the company to handle their money and produce competitive returns. The threats from new entrants into the market are weak.

■ *Threat of substitute products*—it seems that the threat of substitutes is low in this industry. It is a simple and necessary service. Substitutes, such as live brokers on the floor and on phones, are cost inhibitive to many and do not provide an advantage. The price performance of a substitute would not yield a worthy alternative. The threat from substitute products is weak.

■ *Level of competition in an industry*—because the derivatives markets trade such large amounts of money every day, this is a very competitive industry. Having an edge can result in much higher profits. This is a fast paced market and any discrepancies are quickly accounted for in the efficiency of the markets. Competition is increasing as many exchanges are merging and buying each other out, not just locally but internationally as well. Thus, the market can change in a blink of an eye and exchanges are becoming a one stop shop in the offerings of financial products. The level of competition in this industry is very strong.

E-Aspects

Business

Today, market opportunities occur in milliseconds. Trades on CME Globex are executed almost instantly and confirmed back to the customer anywhere in the world. The CME Globex electronic trading platform continues to define the cutting edge of financial trading technology. It is the only platform in the world to offer access to all major asset classes—a full range of interest rate, equity index, foreign exchange, commodity, energy products and real estate products. It serves customers around the globe, virtually around the clock, with high-speed, high-volume capacity, enhanced options, a range of new products and clearing on the world's largest clearing system. The functionality and capacity of the platform have grown dramatically to accommodate the increased demand. With each system enhancement, CME's electronic marketplace has become more efficient and more easily accessible. Every upgrade to the system has led to expanded participation in all markets.

Network Communications and Business Intelligence Technologies

The heart of CME's system is its Globex electronic platform, which combines its electronic functions and floor trader functions into a single cohesive system. This system is the bread and butter of its operations and accounts for a large portion of its business. The information system provides real-time, delayed and historical market data for traders all around the world. CME uses the latest servers, such as blade servers and multi-core processors from leading vendors and suppliers such as Dell, IBM, Intel and AMD. Aside from having the latest hardware, a reliable and fast network is also employed. Networking technologies complement the maximization of throughput and minimize latency of data.

They have dedicated fiber optic lines and deploy the latest networking infrastructure such as Infiniband from Cisco Systems and multi-cast streaming, which is faster than the TCP/IP and UDP protocols that many consumers currently use. Additional consideration must be given to implementation and co-ordination of the entire market data system. Without all the components working together efficiently, the system is only as fast as its slowest component. The slowest component is constantly changing, from hardware to software to the network. Each, at some point in time, presents a bottleneck to the system and as one bottleneck is fixed another pops up.

CME and the financial industry are pushing the limits of current technology and now have explored exotic technologies to address the problem of growing volumes of data. Technologies such as the powerful chips in gaming consoles and the cell processor in the Playstation 3 are being explored to take advantage of their massive computing power. This is just an example of the hardware acceleration technologies.

Developing and implementing technologies such as Infiniband can increase performance by reducing the network overhead and transmitting data more efficiently. Software considerations include the research and development of more efficient data structures and high level languages to have more concise code, which reduces message size and requires less processing. All of these in combination are being researched and implemented into the technology infrastructure of the CME, to make it a model and leader in its industry.

Aside from providing financial market data, CME also provides clearing services and other services to manage risk and test trade automation. The vast amount of information stored in many databases, in which the information can be later retrieved for further analysis and used to perform risk analytics and trade back testing. CME provides accounting and regulatory functions to its customers, eliminating the need for separate systems to perform these functions, and emphasizing CME as a financial services one stop shop.

People Issues

Although this trading system gives participants instant access to market data, equal market access to all participants, and allows clients to manage their own network connection, there are certain people issues that will come with the implementation of this technology. First, this technology may cut jobs for the traditional floor workers on which participants originally depended. As awareness spreads about the CME Internet interface, participants may become more interested in the instantaneous execution benefits and less interested in brokers and other trade assisting employees.

Customers around the world will be expecting high performance and stable, regularly updated data. Another issue to take into consideration is the clutter of data and maintenance problems with the 24-hour system. Positions within the company must be responsible for maintaining or enhancing the existing product line, responding to customer needs, while ensuring the product line is profitable and competitive.

IT Solution Development

The intention is to give the CME a competitive advantage via process speed, so priority is given to the technical specialists to produce the fastest solutions. The system must be designed so that a user can easily navigate through it and execute the trades that they desire, but this must not be at the expense of the process speed.

The systems lifecycle is the oldest method for systems development. It is very structured, with goals and checkpoints that must be met and approved before the system can proceed to the next level; end users are not very involved. When a prototyping approach is used, a rough model is developed to elicit feedback from end users. It is a very interactive development process, and the prototype can be modified and updated as end users find areas that need to be changed.

A drawback is that these prototypes can be hastily developed and they may not be technically ready for production. Another alternative is having the end users develop the system independently or with very little help from the technical specialists. End users can add exactly what they want and design the system to meet their requirements. Since design specialists are not used, the quality of the program and the control of systems may be lacking, as would be the technical expertise to develop a fast and efficient system quickly and efficiently.

The intention of such systems is to eliminate as much of the lag time as possible. As a minimum this is to remain in contention. Ideally these systems help provide competitive advantage.

Security

Maintaining the security of the entire IT system in regards to market information is a daunting task. With thousands of users representing millions of investors, the validity, protection and timeliness of that information is a critical aspect to CME and its stakeholders. The firm must validate the credentials of clients wishing to access data and it must control where and how data is distributed. Data in user accounts must be accurate and safe, with procedures in place to ensure correct crediting and confirmation of trades. Further, the CME has to protect its systems from being hacked into, to prevent disruptions to the market. This could undermine market integrity and have a significant detrimental impact on not only the U.S. economy, but moreover the global economy.

To help ensure market data integrity and price reporting, regulatory bodies such as the United States Securities and Exchange Commission publish guidelines that exchanges must meet in regards to electronic information. Without a standard and guidelines on reporting financial information, the benefits of electronic trading may be mitigated, as the clarity of information may fall and the number of formats may rise, causing confusion in the market.

It is essential to ensure that data is accurate and properly stated and that the systems meet the essential "thresholds" of being online and fully functional. Without these essential criteria, the market becomes inefficient and the CME loses its integrity, which is a key component to its competitive advantage.

Ethical Considerations

The issues related to this system concern matters that, although not illegal, are not ethically accepted practice. By law, the system and its implementation must comply with the rules and regulations on market data set forth by the United States Securities and Exchange Commission and other regulatory bodies worldwide. It is important that organizations provide market data to clients or they will risk violation of governing rules and regulations with possible sanctions.

To better ensure ethical conduct, the company's professional code and code of ethics should be adhered to. All members shall respect one another and present themselves to others in a respectable manner. Lack of group cohesion and respectability creates a tense working environment and can lead to unethical conduct.

There are ethical concerns regarding how customers are treated. For those with margin accounts, customer service and policy can become an issue. Larger, institutional investment firms may be given preferential treatment. They may be called and notified regarding the situation of their accounts. On the other hand, individual investors may have their accounts liquidated to cover their margin call. This may not be ethical, but the holding firms may not be able to afford to give all of their customers this kind of treatment.

Project Management

The transition between the current state of this IT at the CME Group and the proposed change will require vast amounts of hardware and software replacements and, with the massive amount of information flowing through the system, cannot be changed overnight. The Standish Group "Chaos" Report (1995) states that, for IT projects, 31 percent will be cancelled before completed, 53 percent will cost 189 percent of the budget, only 16 percent of software projects were completed within the time and budget constraints, and lastly 50–80 percent of large IS projects, such as this, fail.

It will require months if not years of planning and execution, further justifying the need for thorough and effective project management. Although this project has not come to be a reality yet, when the decision is made to upgrade to pure real-time information streaming, it will require the efficient management of all the knowledge and processes that go into such an ambitious IT implementation. In addition, and more importantly, the expectations and needs of the stakeholders, specifically the CME Group, must be considered at all stages of the project management lifecycle.

Effective project management includes consideration of several key aspects. As already mentioned, the end result must always be kept in mind throughout the entirety of the project. The CME Group will have to consider who this project is going to affect, and how those groups will be affected. Not only will individual traders, brokers and investors be affected but firms which are based on the information that the CME provides will also be affected. The proposed solution will take a lot away from day traders and brokers, and will therefore negatively affect them. However, the speed at which the information will be conveyed throughout the world will benefit the investor as well as any firms accessing the information.

12

Next, the lifecycle of the project will need to be identified: Initiate, Plan, Execute, Control and Close. These are all crucial steps to creating project management that will result in a successful deliverable.

Global Considerations

One of the best examples of the necessity for global considerations is in the financial industry. Stocks, options and commodities are traded throughout the world both globally and locally, which works as a major facilitator in the effectiveness of this solution. Still, there are several barriers that must be identified before attempting a major IT implementation such as this. It is first important to consider that this will be a worldwide system and the information that this system will be outputting must be translatable into a large number of languages.

Additionally, there are major issues with data transferring over borders, in terms of regulatory restrictions, as well as the speed and infrastructure needed to handle the proposed speed. They will need to work directly with organizations that are using their information to ensure that it is conveyed in a manner that is useful to them. In this, one must consider that there are different understandings and translation barriers across different cultures and it is unlikely that everyone will have the same definitions, views and perspectives on things.

The CME Group must also consider the difference in time zones, and when exactly they will be able to perform maintenance, as well as when and how they will be implementing their new solutions. Therefore, all the considerations that have been mentioned in terms of organizations that are using the information must be considered with the people developing. It is essential for CME to remain the world's largest commodities exchange and, in order to maintain that competitive advantage, they must manage the expectations of their stakeholders and work with them to find the best way to implement such a change.

Conclusions and Recommendation

As noted, the CME Group is the world's largest commodities exchange and the transformation of information from close to real-time, to actual real-time information will provide the CME Group with further competitive advantage to distinguish itself from its competitors. It is an age old saying that time is money, and this statement is especially true in financial markets where the first person with information regarding moves in the market will be the first person able to react and, therefore, make money from the said move. Providing the most up-to-date information, in turn, will enable CME to provide its users with the highest value. The challenge for CME is to ensure that they continue to do this.

Case Exercise References

Gerlach, D. (2007), What is a Stock?, www.youngmoney.com/investing/sharebuilder/goals/031021_10.

Leinweber, D.J. (2002) Using Information from Trading in Trading and Portfolio Management: Ten Years Later, Working Papers 1135, California Institute of Technology, Division of the Humanities and Social Sciences.

McDowall, B. (2005) Algorithmic Trading: Its Growth and Limitations, www.it-analysis.com/business/content.php?cid=8236.

Townsend Analytics (2007) Corporate Overview, www.townsendanalytics.com.

The Economist (2007) Ahead of the Tape, www.economist.com/finance/displaystory.cfm?story_id=9370718.

The Economist (2006) Technology and Exchanges, www.economist.com/finance/displaystory.cfm?story_id= E1_VQSVPRT.

The Trade (2005) A Buy-Side Handbook Algorithmic Trading, www.thetradenews.com/files/magazine/algo_1.pdf.

Case Exercise Questions

1   What is the role for KM in this context?

2   Specifically, outline how both tacit knowledge and explicit knowledge would provide CME with a sustainable competitive advantage.

3   What are the key people, process and technology considerations in CME that are relevant to KM?

4   What strategies would you recommend to foster a KM culture in this setting?

FURTHER READING

Davenport, T. and Prusak, L. (1998) *Working Knowledge*. Boston, MA: Harvard Business School Press.

Lehaney, B., Clarke, S., Coakes, E., and Jack, G. (2004*) Beyond Knowledge Management*. Hershey, PA: Idea Group Publishing.

Liebowitz, J. (2008) *Making Cents out of Knowledge Management*. Lanham, MD: The Scarecrow Press.

Wickramasinghe, N. and von Lubitz, D. (2007) *Knowledge-based Enterprise Theories and Fundamentals*. Hershey, PA: IGI.

Wigg, K. (1993) *Knowledge Management Foundations*. Arlington, VA: Schema Press.

REFERENCES

Alavi, M. (2000) Managing Organizational Knowledge, in R.W. Zmud (Ed.), *Framing the Domains of IT Management*. Cincinnati, OH: Pinnaflex Educational Resources, pp. 15–28.

Boland, R. and Tenkasi, R. (1995) Perspective Making Perspective Taking, *Organization Science*, 6: 350–372.

Davenport, T. and L. Prusak (1998) *Working Knowledge*. Boston, MA: Harvard Business School Press.

Dervin, B. (1988) Sense Making Theory and Practice: An Overview of User Interests in Knowledge Seeking and Use, *Knowledge Management*, 2:2, MCB University Press, December.

Drucker, P. (1993) *Post-Capitalist Society*. New York: HarperCollins.

Drucker, P. (1999) Beyond the Information Revolution, *The Atlantic Monthly*, October: 47–57.

Grant, R. (1991) The Resource-Based Theory of Competitive Advantage: Implications for Strategy Formulation, *California Management Review*, 33(3) Spring: 114–135.

Hedlund, G. (1990) A Model of Knowledge Management and the N-Form Corporation, *Strategic Management Journal*, 15: 73–90.

Hope, J. and Hope, T. (1997) *Competing in the Third Wave*. Boston, MA: Harvard Business School Press.

Huber, G. (1990). A Theory of the Effects of Advanced Information Technologies on Organizational Design, Intelligence, and Decision Making, *Academy of Management Review*, 15(1): 47–71.

Ichijo, K. and Nonaka, I. (2007) *Knowledge Creation and Management*. Oxford: Oxford University Press.

Jafari, M., Fathian, M., Jahani, A., and Akhavan, P. (2008) Exploring the Contextual Dimensions of Organization from Knowledge Management Perspective, *VINE* 38(1): 53–71.

Kanter, J. (1999). Knowledge Management Practically Speaking, *Information Systems Management*, 16(4): 7–16.

Liebowitz, J. (1999) *Knowledge Management Handbook*. London: CRC Press.

Malhotra, Y. (2000) Knowledge Management and New Organizational Forms, in Y. Malhotra (Ed.), *Knowledge Management and Virtual Organizations*. Hershey, PA: Idea Group Publishing, pp. 35–48.

Nonaka, I. (1991) The Knowledge Creating Company, in *Harvard Business Review on Knowledge Management* (1998). Boston, MA: Harvard Business School Press, pp. 21–32.

Nonaka, I. (1994) A Dynamic Theory of Organizational Knowledge Creation, *Organization Science*, 5: 14–37.

Prahalad, C. and Hamel, G. (1990) *The Core Competence of the Corporation*. Boston, MA: Harvard Business School Press.

Polayni, M. (1958) *Personal Knowledge: Towards a Post-Critical Philosophy*. Chicago, IL: The University of Chicago Press.

Polayni, M. (1966) *The Tacit Dimension*. London: Routledge & Kegan Paul.

Shapiro, C. and Varian, H. (1999) *Information Rules*. Boston, MA: Harvard Business School Press.

Snowden, D. (2005) Multi-Ontology Sense Making: A New Simplicity in Decision Making. Available online at www.cognitive-edge.com/ceresources/articles/40_Multi-ontology_sense_m akingv2_May05.pdf (accessed July 19, 2008).

Standish Group (1995) "Chaos" Report. Available online at www.net.educause.edu/ir/library/pdf/NCP08083B.pdf (assessed January 12, 2009).

Swan, J., Scarbrough, H., and Preston, J. (1999) Knowledge Management—The Next Fad To Forget People?, Proceedings of the 7th European Conference in Information Systems, Copenhagen: Copenhagen Business School, pp. 668–678.

Weick, Karl E. (1995) *Sensemaking in Organizations*. Thousand Oaks, CA: Sage.

Wickramasinghe, N. and von Lubitz, D. (2007) *Knowledge-Based Enterprise Theories and Fundamentals*. Hershey, PA: IGI.

Wigg, K. (1993) *Knowledge Management Foundations*. Arlington, VA: Schema Press.

Zack, M. (1999) *Knowledge and Strategy*. Boston, MA: Butterworth Heinemann.

Chapter 2

Knowledge Strategies and Knowledge Capture

INTRODUCTION

As discussed in the previous chapter, KM helps organizations attain or maintain sustainable competitive advantage. This chapter discusses knowledge management strategies. It provides a brief background to strategy, and develops arguments as to why and how strategy can relate strongly to KM, and how one can inform the other. Strategy is about long-term planning, but it is meaningless unless objectives are clear. Organizational culture is something that is slow to change, therefore strategic thinking involves considering not just what financial and technical changes may be needed, but also the human factors that may affect outcomes.

It is important that KM is not viewed by managers as a short-term project, and that it is seen as contributing to strategy. KM, however, is in itself not a strategic objective, and there is no end state. It is ongoing and should be viewed as an integral part of the organization. For it to be successful, it must be embedded in the culture, as is the case for quality.

Although technological development may be positive, it may also bring disadvantages. For example, the increase in technology has increased virtual contact and reduced the opportunity for face-to-face debate and conceptualization, possibly leading to the loss of tacit knowledge. It is, therefore, the setting up of appropriate and balanced systems to develop and implement KM that is derived from and informs strategy that remains difficult.

Bali and Dwivedi (2004) explore organizational culture and the implementation of management information systems, introducing the Management Information System Culture-Organization, which combines the intangible requirements of culture change with the implementation of a new IT system. In both cases the importance of balance can be recognized.

Conversely, even with the highest specification technology in place, without the appropriate management style, culture and processes to embed the concept of KM, a holistic KM strategy would be difficult to implement, hence the importance of balance, as argued by Dwivedi *et al.* (2005). They produced a holistic KM framework for healthcare institutions, within which they recognized the importance of integrating information communication technology and knowledge sharing, stating that healthcare institutions needed to "identify key sociological and technological roles" to achieve the culture change necessary to improve efficiency.

In Western economies, organizations have seen huge changes to both domestic and world trade. KM has become more relevant as the nature of Western economies has shifted from manufacturing to services. In a service-oriented economy, knowledge, rather than physical assets, is at a premium. In recent years there have been shifts from traditional, highly structured organizations, to more fluid businesses in areas as diverse as manufacturing, healthcare, entertainment and education.

Knowledge creation, sharing and retention are the keys to gaining and retaining competitive edge in this dynamic environment. Organizations could choose to let their knowledge be treated in an ad hoc fashion, or manage the asset "knowledge" in a way that would lever the best value of it and treat it as a prime resource that needs to be managed at a strategic level. This means considering how KM may help achieve organizational goals, how it may influence such goals, how knowledge may be acquired (intelligence gathering) and how knowledge assets may be measured.

CAPTURING KNOWLEDGE

Given the accepted existence of two types of knowledge (explicit and tacit), this section deals with how one can effectively capture tacit knowledge. This is because explicit knowledge has already been captured in the form of its current state (i.e. in the form of reports, charts and other documentation). Tacit knowledge is often much harder to capture as this may reside in the form of "expertise" (some authors refer to this as knowledge that may be "trapped" in somebody's head).

To demonstrate how aspects of KM have perhaps been used *avant la lettre*, most companies operate the practice of carrying out an "exit interview" with employees who are leaving an organization. This usually takes the form of a questionnaire and interview where the company tries to find out the reasons for the employee's departure. Patterns can often be detected if several employees provide the same or similar reasons. It may, however, be argued that even this is a case of too little, too late. The employee has, after all, still left (along with his or her knowledge).

Other common, effective and obvious ways of capturing knowledge include the use of qualitative and quantitative research methods, such as questionnaires, interviews and observation. The use of interviews is to be encouraged since questionnaires often only allow for a limited or "fixed" range of opinions (for example, yes/no answers or ranking-based questions which do not allow for variation, however slight—and yet important—this may be). A yes/no option does not allow for the answer "well, sometimes," which could be crucial.

KM-based innovations, such as social networks and wikis, also enable organizations to efficiently gather facts and opinions. It could be argued that the "social" nature of such knowledge capture enables the organization to garner opinions and knowledge that may otherwise remain inaccessible.

Finally, simple "brainstorming" techniques can be very effective ways of gathering tacit knowledge. In a group environment such techniques can help participants to focus their ideas and trigger new thoughts, while working with the thrust of a team. The resulting thoughts and opinions can then be used as a basis for refinement. Other terms that are used for "brainstorming" include mind shower, mind map, word storm, brain dump, word dump, thought dump or round robin.

ORGANIZING KNOWLEDGE: A STRATEGIC VIEW

Skyrme and Amidon (1997) suggest six different types of knowledge, building on the five questions: how, who, when, where, why, but also including a final category, "that":

1 *Know-how* is the knowledge of how to get things done, and some of this knowledge is made explicit in organizational procedures, but in practice much of it is tacit and in people's heads.
2 *Know-who* is about knowing who can help, and this relies on the ability to appreciate other people's skills and strengths (and weaknesses). Knowing who not to ask is also very important.
3 *Know-when* is about sense of timing. For example, skilled stock market operators seem to have the knack of buying when everybody else is selling.
4 *Know-where* is about knowing where things are best carried out. This arises in localities where people with certain skills congregate—places like silicone valley for high technology or the City of London or New York for international finance.
5 *Know-why* is about the wider context and vision. This knowledge allows individuals to do what is right for a customer rather than slavishly following a procedure.
6 *Know-that* is the basic sense of knowing. It represents accepted facts but also experience and access to learning. A skilled mechanic may know that the cause of a problem is likely to be found in a particular component.

Sveiby (2006) splits KM initiatives into three areas: External Structure Initiatives (ESIs), Internal Structure Initiatives (ISIs) and Competence Initiatives (CIs). ESIs involve gaining knowledge from customers or suppliers and offering knowledge to customers or suppliers. For example, from 1982 General Electric (GE) (U.S.) has collected all customer complaints in a database that supports telephone operators in answering customer calls, and GE has programmed 1.5 million potential problems and their solutions into its system. The National Bicycle Industrial Company (Japan) produces bicycles that are tailored to each customer's height, weight and color choice, and this is done in a single day, by means of their customer database being integrated with computer aided design and computer integrated manufacturing. Agro Corp (U.S.) sells seed and fertilizers, and assists farmer's choices by analyzing data on their soils together with weather forecasts and information on crops.

Sveiby's (2006) Internal Structure Initiatives include things such as building a knowledge sharing culture and creating new revenues from existing resources. Examples include Outokumppu (Finland), which uses knowledge on how to build smelting plants to educate staff of customers throughout the world, with the result that this is now bigger business than the original smelting activity. Skandia (Switzerland) has a back office system that is now sold to Swiss insurance companies.

Sveiby's (2006) Competence Initiatives include creating careers based on KM and creating microenvironments for the transfer of tacit knowledge. Examples are Buckman Labs (USA) where employees gain financial rewards and higher positions for knowledge sharing, and Affärsvärlden (Sweden), where team writing and piggy-backing are used to help new journalists develop more quickly.

Probst *et al.* (2000) view KM as a process that encompasses knowledge identification, knowledge acquisition, knowledge sharing and knowledge utilization. Knowledge may be considered as tacit or explicit, and this categorization is often attributed to Nonaka and Takeuchi (1995) but Polanyi (1962) is considered by many to be the original source. Explicit or codified knowledge is transmittable in formal systematic language. Tacit knowledge is personal, context specific and therefore hard to formalize and communicate. Other views of organizational knowledge include the traditional hierarchical approach of data, information, knowledge and wisdom. Yet another view is of organizational knowledge as being at the cusp of people, processes and technology.

The foregoing outline provides high-level views of knowledge and how it may be organized. The following sections discuss intelligence gathering and measuring the value of knowledge.

INTELLIGENCE GATHERING

Knowledge-based systems need to acquire various forms of knowledge, which includes knowledge of what exists and what does not (declarative knowledge—"know that") and processes (procedures—"know what," "know where," "know who," "know how"). Declarative knowledge is about facts, concepts and inference. Procedural knowledge is about rules, methods and documented organizational norms. Facts and concepts are often general in nature, while rules and methods tend to be specific to particular tasks. For example, a design engineer at an automobile plant would need to know the processes required to take an initial idea through to production.

Intelligence gathering (knowledge capture), for a knowledge-based system, links closely to concepts from expert systems, in which attempts are made to transform the knowledge of an expert into something that will be available to others. As mentioned in the previous section, one view of knowledge is that it can be divided into tacit and explicit. Explicit knowledge is relatively easily identified and codified. The challenge that still faces those engaged in KM is that the most valuable knowledge is tacit, and such knowledge is notoriously difficult to identify and to codify. Tacit knowledge is to do with "gut feel." It may be exemplified by the years of built-in experience of a senior consultant cardiologist who makes a life or death decision about a patient.

Experts are not always able to explain exactly why they have made decisions, and are therefore not necessarily able to provide the rules for such decisions. Their expertise is rare and valuable, and we put our trust in doctors, mechanics, technicians, engineers, lawyers and accountants. At lower levels, many people are able to grasp at least the fundamentals of these subject areas, but as issues become more complicated, deep and layered, most of us do not have the experience, knowledge or ability to be experts in all of these fields.

It is therefore challenging to attempt to gain knowledge from an expert, without the additional complication of transforming that knowledge into something that can be coded and shared with others. An expert might relate anecdotes or examples, but without supplying clear rules to establish patterns, it is not possible to transfer such intelligence to a knowledge-based system. Even further, experts may, in their attempts to explain tacit knowledge, inadvertently give misleading information. In addition, five experts may give five different views on a particular case, and this leads to a view of knowledge acquisition as something that evolves. One major challenge with this is that evolution can take considerable time.

The term "intelligence" has traditionally been used by military organizations to refer to information that has been evaluated in some way or another. It is about value (

relevance), as opposed to data, which is often evaluated in terms of accuracy and detail. Thus, intelligence is more than data and more than information, and intelligence may be equated with knowledge. It relates to context and meaning, and must therefore be current and relevant to the issues being considered.

Private and public sector organizations have begun to recognize the value of intelligence, though, initially, this was almost solely in the realm of what was then called industrial espionage. That is, spying on competitors in order to find out what their latest developments are and using this information to gain or retain competitive edge. Within organizations in today's world, intelligence gathering has other, less sinister meanings.

By way of example: there are many means of gathering intelligence. Standard searches of published material may be used to find out such things as the size of companies, their turnover, etc. Concomitantly, other approaches may be used to collect original data. These might include questionnaire surveys, individual interviews, group interviews, focus groups and other well-known approaches. A KMS would attempt to incorporate automated intelligence gathering and would try to share this where appropriate. Examples of this include organizational "yellow pages" and web folders for project teams.

MEASURING

One of the challenging areas within KM is concerned with measurement. Organizations use various strategies for value creation to attain high performance that creates profit, growth and competitive positions. Creativity is a key concept in KM. It is about developing things in new ways, adapting existing practices and finding a competitive edge by being different from rival organizations. Creativity is an example of an intangible, and it is an example of the use of knowledge held by individuals and groups. An intangible is something that cannot be touched. Intangibles are nonetheless valuable, and in today's world, possibly more valuable than tangible assets.

A part of intangible assets is intellectual capital, and some authors refer to intellectual bandwidth; that is, the ability of an organization to create value with its intellectual capital. Intellectual capital may be thought of as the non-physical and non-monetary assets that are

Table 2.1 *Sample Intelligence Gathering Questions*

What is the age profile of customers?

How many members of staff hold degrees?

Who is the expert in the organization on X?

How much is spent on a particular form of promotion and what returns does that bring?

If the organization is to develop to meet the challenges it will face in five years time, what training programs will be needed, who will run them, what will they cost, and which members of staff should participate?

What are the likely trends within our market?

How will the economic downturn affect our competitors?

What do particular demographic changes mean to our organization?

held by an organization. Traditionally, intangibles were considered as either not measurable or too difficult to measure. With the recognition that knowledge is a prime asset, or possibly the only asset, this has had to change. The challenge is to find ways to measure such things and to achieve agreed standards. Currently, that debate is still being held, and the following discussions outline a number of factors related to these issues.

The MERITUM Project (2002) was funded by the European Union to prepare guidelines for measuring intangible assets. This suggests that management organizes both critical and non-critical intangibles through knowledgeable activities to meet organizational objectives. In doing this, the organization will concomitantly engage in the value creation process.

Mehta (2007) suggests three knowledge types: core knowledge (minimum for the firm to be in the business); advanced knowledge (for competitive viability); and innovative knowledge (to enable competitive advantage). Mehta (2007) continues by highlighting the importance of assessing value and developing direct, as well as indirect, measures of value assessment. The importance of this is more to do with the overall value of the organization than a single year's profit margin.

Mehta (2007) highlights the importance of a number of factors that help make a KM strategy effective in the value creation process. These are: articulating the KM strategy; helping the organization define the KM strategy in the light of corporate strategy; facilitating knowledge flows; helping to improve knowledge flow and build appropriate human and technical infrastructures; enabling innovation; realigning an organization's institutional structures to address strategic knowledge gaps; assessing value; and developing direct as well as indirect measures of value assessment. This is associated with a view that an organization's worth is to do with direct and indirect measures to assess economic, social, intellectual and cultural value created within and outside the organization.

CASE EXERCISE: PROBLEM UNDERSTANDING IN THE EAST SLOVAKIA COAL INDUSTRY

This case is drawn from Lehaney et al. (2008)

The initial issues in this case were to do with physical processes, and a particular manager wanted to improve production. In fact, the case turned out to relate more to strategy, operations management in a wider sense, information flows and culture. The investigation revealed misunderstandings and poor communication that created resource waste.

The manager had difficulties in meeting targets set by the marketing department. He had tried to use forecasting, without much success, and wondered if simulating the processes would be of help, and if some combination of approaches would be useful. What was clear was that the management desire was for a technical solution, and it was apparent that issues such as culture and knowledge sharing were not initially on the management agenda. Plant managers wanted quantitative models and quantifiable solutions.

The Upper Nitra Basin is the richest and largest brown coal basin in Slovakia and Upper Nitra Mines (UNM) was founded on July 1, 1996 by the transformation of a former state-owned set of mines. Under state planning, coal demand was highly stable. Mine managers were told what to produce, and there was no necessity to change production, since demand was secured by government order. After the fall of Communism (in 1989), UNM faced the new and uncertain conditions of the free market. UNM was forced to renew all previous sales contracts and try to win customers within the market under competition.

In this new situation, the newly formed Czech Republic suddenly became a competitor, as did other East European coal producers such as Poland and Ukraine. Piped Russian gas began to be delivered cheaply to increasing numbers of homes throughout Slovakia. In the face of such competition UNM has had to re-evaluate its situation and decide if it is willing and able to find new markets, or at what points it should downsize, and possibly close. The effect of closure would be multiplied across East Slovakia, as direct and knock-on employment in many areas depends upon the coalmines. Currently there is no possibility of alternative employment, since the Russian piped gas requires relatively few local operatives and the Slovakian government is unwilling or unable to provide further financial assistance.

Gas heating installation in villages has been growing rapidly, to replace traditional coal heating. The gas heating is as cheap as or cheaper than coal heating, but is clean, easily controlled, and the gas may also be used for cooking. In addition, unlike the past when village youngsters worked locally on the land or in mines, today's young people are moving into towns and cities to seek employment. This reduces local demand for coal, and the central heating systems of the cities tend to use gas or electricity.

District heating is the dominant method of heat supply in Slovakia, where almost 100 percent of city accommodation is supplied with heat from district heating, which represents approximately 49 percent of all the households in Slovakia. Approximately 39 percent of primary energy source consumption is used for heat production in industry, service sectors and households either for space heating or for production purposes. The fuel base of district heating plants includes mainly natural gas (71.3 percent), followed by coal (16.4 percent), fuel oil (6.7 percent) and others (5.6 percent). Approximately 970,000 households are supplied by individual heating, of which 870,000 households are family houses with electric heating, coal stoves, gas ovens or wood stoves.

There are three major companies, located in five different regions, producing coal in the Slovak Republic. The first and the major one is the Upper Nitra Mines (UNM), which has three subsidiaries: Mine Cigel, Mine Handlova and Mine Novaky. The second is Mine Dolina and the third is Mine Zahorie. These three companies in the year 2004 employed 8,774 people and produced 3.746 million tonnes of coal. The Novaky electric power station is the only one in the Slovak Republic that passes Western European emission standards. Novaky used over 2.5 million tonnes of coal in 2004. Households and communities used 618 thousand tonnes of assorted sized coal and the bulk of the remainder was used by the chemical industry.

With a skilled and competitively priced labor force, strong manufacturing tradition and proximity to European markets, Slovakia's prospects may appear to be favorable. Previously state-controlled sectors, such as energy (coal, gas), have now been opened to competition, however, and raw materials firms can no longer rely on obtaining long-term government contracts. In the light of this competition, information flows and information management are now extremely important. In these new, unstable and dynamically changing conditions, managers need effective decision support methods and ways to reconsider their systems so that market advantages can be realized in production and sales.

Historically, the Production Manager had been told to process as much coal as was delivered from the mines. In the new market environment he would have liked to know what demand existed, for which products, in what timescales, and be able to react to these and be proactive in the processing operation. Coal that is processed and not bought by the market on the same day has a very short life span and thus is waste product. Although having moved to a market situation, the processing plant continued to be managed as if in a planned economy. Regardless of market demand, the mine produced coal to levels that relate purely to current ability to produce. This coal is taken to the processing facility, which is forced to receive all coal from the mine.

The market requires specific amounts of coal of different assortments, and the processing manager is under enormous pressure to meet this demand, yet currently there is no direct link between market demand and coal production at the mine. The authors proposed that the process would work much more effectively if mine production were influenced directly by market demand. While in a market economy this suggestion might be seen as obvious, it was a suggestion against the culture. Nevertheless, it was difficult for those who resisted to offer rational arguments against the proposal.

Those who resisted were, however, in the majority and strongly influenced decisions. Eventually, after much debate, it was agreed that if it could be shown that the proposed model would be more efficient, it would be adopted. A proxy for improved efficiency that was agreed was the amount of waste coal produced. It was also agreed that a simulation model should be developed to demonstrate the effects of the proposed new policy. The model showed vast improvements in reducing physical coal waste, and this was as a direct result of market knowledge feeding into information flows. The value of this knowledge may be estimated by the cost savings that were due to the reduction of coal waste.

The structure of various units and their interactions with each other were the primary issues that needed to be addressed. The key change was when participants began to discover more about their own systems, and to realize that the issue of information management is vital in addressing this situation. Thus, what had started out as a possibly straightforward operational research modeling situation, became an intervention in which the major issues were ones of cultural change and management of information.

Despite the demonstrated advantages for operational planning, successful implementation would require some strategic changes, altering established practices and relationships with other segments of the company, in particular with the coal extraction site and marketing division. The proposed scenario has been discussed extensively and it clearly demonstrates improvement by using forecast market demand rather than fixed deliveries dictated by the mine. This approach requires an investment in culture change, in modeling and in information management. While everyone at the mine accepts the logic of the solution, there is still huge resistance to change, and this resistance comes from some of the more senior management.

As the case developed, the issues of information management and the necessity to change existing practices highlighted the personal, strategic, cultural and societal issues. After exploring the problem situation it became apparent that the Production Manager's problem was not one of the need for modeling techniques, but one of change management. In order to further that case, he needed to demonstrate the value of market knowledge. All the information needed to address the issues was available, but the organization and its information flows had to be considered in new ways if the issues were to be addressed successfully.

Malhotra (2003) addresses the complexity of measuring intangibles and defines intellectual capital as wealth creating knowledge, information, intellectual property and experience. Lehaney *et al.* (2004) argue that intellectual capital, including creativity knowledge sharing, affects the organization's market value overall, but not necessarily the tangibles of profit margins. This is a key point, and it should be noted that if share values were directly related to profits per annum, they would be easy to predict. In fact, the share market is what is known as a "random walk," and predicting share values is notoriously difficult. There is some relationship with profit margins, but the long-term value of shares is more closely linked with the perception of an organization's value.

A knowledge-based organization typically has intellectual capital as its major asset but typically this value is usually not declared in annual reports and does not appear in conventional analysis models. The Danish Government has attempted to address this issue over a number of years, and has produced guidelines for intellectual capital evaluation (Danish Agency for Trade and Industry, 2000). This report indicates that:

> The intellectual capital statement supports the company's knowledge management, i.e. the part of management work that obtains, shares, develops and anchors knowledge resources. The intellectual capital statement provides a status of the company's efforts to develop its knowledge resources through knowledge management in text, figures and illustrations.
>
> The intellectual capital statement is both a strategic tool for adding value to the company and a communication tool for inducing employees, customers and others to engage in this process. The intellectual capital statement thus points to the future and is not primarily intended to account for the current portfolio of knowledge resources at any particular time.
>
> The objective of an intellectual capital statement is not to calculate the value of the company's knowledge in financial terms. Also, this is probably not feasible. Thus, an intellectual capital statement cannot be used to explain the difference between a company's book value and its market value, although this is sometimes the stated purpose of intellectual capital statements. Such use of the statement is for several reasons meaningless. Firstly, the difference would depend on accounting standards and on market developments generally. Secondly, it would require that the market already knew the true value of the company, thus eliminating the need for calculating this.
>
> (p. 3)

The intellectual capital statement consists of three elements: a knowledge narrative, KM challenges and KM reporting. The knowledge narrative outlines how a company meets customer's requirements, and specifies how the company has organized its resources to achieve this. KM challenges are defined from the knowledge narrative. They should be translated into actions for implementing the objectives that derive from the knowledge narrative. The report is informed by the knowledge narrative and the KM challenges.

Text, figures and illustrations are used for the external intellectual capital statement, which is the document reporting on the company strategy for KM. Text relates to the knowledge narrative, the management challenges and the specific actions. Figures document the initiatives launched to address management challenges, with actions tied to indicators. Illustrations may be photographs, charts or any graphical depictions that help to communicate the knowledge narrative and the KM challenges, and that aid the reader to gain an impression of the organization's style, character and identity (Danish Agency for Trade and Industry, 2000).

The *Skandia Navigator* model is one of the first approaches to be used in this area, and its initial internal intellectual capital report was based upon the basis proposed by Edvinsson and Malone (1997). This model divides the intellectual capital of an organization into three forms: human capital, structural capital and customer capital. Human capital includes staff competence, capabilities, skills, experiences, creativity and innovation. The infrastructure is provided by structural capital and it includes organizational processes, procedures, technologies, information sources and intellectual property rights. It may be argued that the organizational physical environment is a major factor within this. Customer capital may relate to good will, and is related to an organization's relationships with its customers, suppliers, trade and professional associations and any external links.

The *Balanced Scorecard* (Kaplan and Norton, 1996) has four general perspectives, and these are financial, customer, internal process, and learning and growth. The financial perspective considers an organization's strategy and how that contributes to profits. It incorporates the tangible outcomes of the strategy in traditional financial terms. The customer addresses the value proposition that the organization chooses to apply in order to satisfy customers and generate additional sales to the most desired customers. The internal process perspective considers processes that create and deliver the customer value proposition. It focuses on activities that are needed for an organization to provide, effectively and efficiently, value expected by customers. The learning and growth perspective links strongly to KM and is the basis of developing and increasing the intangible assets of an organization, with its focus on internal skills and capabilities that are required to support value-creating processes.

Accounting and financial measurement techniques not only tend to take a historical perspective but also focus on physical or tangible assets. Given that most of KM is concerned with intangible assets, this poses a significant problem. More recently, various attempts to measure the benefits of intangible assets have been developed, including trying to value brands, trademarks and patents.

Skyrme (2005) identified approximately thirty different methods used by companies to try to measure the value of KM. These methods tend to focus on one of the following four areas:

1 valuing knowledge as an asset, potentially tradable;
2 focusing on the benefits of a KM program;
3 assessing KM effectiveness as a basis for year-on-year comparison; and
4 focusing on performance measurement.

There are other approaches to valuing and reporting intangible assets. In many ways these are variations on those discussed previously. They include the Intangible Assets Monitor (Sveiby, 1997), the IC-Index Model (Roos *et al.*, 1997), the Holistic Value Approach (Roos *et al.*, 2005), and the Technology Broker Model (Brooking, 1996). Other measurement models include Tobin's Q, Economic Value Added, Market-to-Book Value, Intellectual Asset Valuation, Total Value Creation, Knowledge Capital Earnings and Citation Weighted Patents.

While all offer various, often similar, ways to evaluate intangibles, there is no commonly agreed approach as yet. Given the myriad of systems currently developed or being developed, it is clear that there is no one unified and agreed upon method to measure knowledge at this time and this is indeed an area that requires further development.

CONCLUSIONS AND SUMMARY

This chapter discussed strategies related to organizing, gathering and measuring knowledge. Strategy is a long-term concept and involves not just traditional financial concepts, but also human dimensions, including organizational culture. KM needs to address strategic aims and to contribute to them, but as KM is not in itself a strategic objective (such as increasing market share), it has to be treated as integral to working practices and embedded in organizational culture, as is the case for quality.

A holistic approach is needed if KM is to be addressed seriously and implemented successfully. Technology may be useful in this, but it must be accompanied by an appropriate management style. Culture and processes are major aspects of KM initiatives.

The decline of manufacturing and the increase of services have been major influences in considering knowledge as a prime asset. To get the best of that asset it has to be managed and evaluated. Knowledge organization, gathering and measurement are important in gaining and retaining competitive edge. It is accepted that, in general, intellectual capital comprises non-monetary and non-physical assets that add value to an organization. There is still no generally agreed approach to evaluating such assets.

REVIEW QUESTIONS

1   Why is knowledge now considered a prime asset in Western economies?

2   What are the main models of organizing knowledge discussed in this chapter?

3   What is the difference between declarative knowledge and procedural knowledge?

4   What challenges arise in trying to capture tacit knowledge?

5   What is the Balanced Scorecard?

6   What is the Skandia Navigator?

DISCUSSION QUESTIONS

1   What is the difference between the value of an organization and the profits it makes?

2   Consider a public sector provision, such as health services in the UK, and a private sector commercial organization. Would both be interested in evaluating organizational knowledge? Why? How would they differ?

3   If knowledge is valuable, what issues are there in trying to create a knowledge sharing culture?

4   Think of an example of a work situation, past, present or that could arise, in which organizing, gathering and evaluating knowledge would be relevant.

CASE EXERCISE: AMAZON[2]

Amazon.com is competing in a growing Internet marketplace that emphasizes competition. The bargaining power of buyers is strong due to the increasing number of Internet retailers, or e-tailers. The suppliers have substantial bargaining power due to the rivalries from current competitors and to the opportunities that are available for potential competitors to launch their own websites. Rivalry is a strong force in this industry as well. Everyone is striving to have the lowest prices and to be number one within the industry.

Amazon also has a strong threat of substitution. Instead of buying, potential customers can borrow from the library, rent from the local video store and download their favorite music from file sharing sites such as Napster or other various MP3 sites. There are, however, many opportunities, including the growth of the economy, new technology that enables consumers to shop at home, and the rise in popularity of personal computers.

Amazon uses technology to offer services that traditional stores cannot match. By using its four core values (convenience, selection, service and price), Amazon uses its skilled and committed staff members to meet or exceed its customers' needs. Amazon has a good competitive advantage over companies in the same industry; nevertheless, they need to address some of the weaknesses that could affect future performance. Some of the weaknesses include high reliance on Internet and e-mail services, weak profit after adding music stores, shipment lead-time and high cost of employment.

Amazon.com has established itself as a strong leader in e-commerce. The current program they have in England and Germany has shown great success and there are plans on continuing to strive and expand their system to support more places abroad. They have also expanded their product offering to include such items as consumer electronics, video games, movie/DVDs, toys and software. By doing this they may enhance the scope of their current products and service offerings.

The threats and weaknesses faced by Amazon.com are definitely hurdles in their path to success. They face many challenges and roadblocks. Among them, aggressive, capable and well-funded competition; the growth challenges and execution risk associated with their own expansion; and the need for large, continuing investments to meet an expanding market opportunity. However, online bookselling and online commerce in general has proven to be a very large market and Amazon.com has established a niche to become one of the most promising and prosperous e-tailers.

Company Introduction

During the summer of 1994, a man named John Bezos, a computer science and electrical-engineering graduate from Princeton University was intrigued when he heard an Internet statistic stating that its usage was growing at 2,300 percent a year. His reaction: This was his wake up call; he then knew what he wanted to do—create an Internet superstore. He left his job at D.E. Shaw and started to draw a list of possible products that he could sell through the Internet. He quickly narrowed his prospects to music and books. Although both products shared a potential advantage for online sales, the music industry would have been a challenge since there were only six major record companies and they had the power to control the distribution of records and CDs sold throughout the U.S. With such control, these firms had the potential to lock out a new business threatening the traditional record store format. On the contrary, Bezos saw a major opportunity to sell books online since there were far too many titles for a single store to stock. There statistics were as follows:

- 1.5 million English language books in print.
- 3 million books in all languages worldwide.
- Largest physical bookstore in the world carried only 175,000 titles.
- 4,200 U.S. publishers.
- The two biggest booksellers: Barnes & Nobles and Borders Group Inc. accounted for less than 12 percent of total sales.

Because of these statistics, Bezos decided to create an online bookstore. Amazon.com opened its virtual doors in July 1995 with a mission to use the Internet to transform book buying into the fastest, easiest and most enjoyable shopping experience possible. Its goal: *To want people to come to Amazon.com, find whatever they want, discover things they did not know they wanted, and leave feeling they have a new favorite place to shop.* Amazon.com's corporate philosophy is simple: If it is good for our customers, it is worth doing. In addition, that is what they did. As word about Amazon.com spread quickly across the Internet, sales picked up rapidly.

Since 1995, Amazon.com has been growing at a rapid pace. It has attracted over 3 million customers from 160 countries with its: 2.5 million book catalog, twenty-four hours a day service, global presence, product expansion and customer focus. Amazon.com has not only been a success throughout the U.S. but internationally as well. While their customer base and product offerings have grown considerably since their early days, Amazon.com is still maintaining their founding commitment to customer satisfaction and the delivery of an educational and inspiring customer experience.

Corporate Strategy

Amazon's strategy is to maximize long-run profitability by entailing diversification into new business areas (books—music—videos) and to achieve this through acquisitions with other online companies.

Figure A *Amazon timeline.*

Problems

Although Amazon.com has been an Internet success, they have encountered some problems. These problems are:

- Barnes & Nobles and Borders Books & Music are currently purchasing 90 percent of their titles directly from publishers—creating an advantage over Amazon.com since Amazon.com is currently purchasing its titles through warehouses.
- Readers are borrowing instead of buying (95 percent of titles sell less than 20,000 copies, of this number 55 percent of them are purchased by libraries).
- The decreasing of mail order books because of the growth of large discount sale retailers.
- Because they have added music to our online store, they are now competing against online books and music stores.
- Experiencing weak profits after expanding to music—they are currently looking at a no-margin and a low-margin base.
- Continuance of high competition within the industry—especially with competitors such as Barnes & Nobles and Borders Books & Music.
- Too much money being spent on advertising—in June 1998, $26.5m was spent on marketing, in which this had only accounted for 23 percent of sales in 1998.

External Analysis

Evaluating a company's external environment means considering the industry's influence based on their performance. This is very important because a company must either mold its strategies to the external factors that affect it or force the industry to change. Amazon.com is in a unique position because although all of its sales are conducted online, it is also competing against very large brick and mortar retail stores. Prior to the entrance of Amazon, the industry was in a mature stage. There were few price wars against competitors. The oligopoly would soon be turned upside down by the entrance of Amazon, Borders and Barnes & Noble.

We will begin the external analysis by considering Porter's Five Competitive Forces and then finish the SWOT analysis by discussing other opportunities and threats Amazon faced.

Porter's Five Forces

1. The risk of new entry by potential competitors is somewhat high because of the ease of entry for an Internet start-up. However, it was because of Amazon's brand name, customer base, and low prices that made it nearly impossible for a company to enter at their level.
2. The degree of rivalry among established companies within an industry is high.
3. The customers have some bargaining power. Rivalry within the industry has started a price war, and customers can force companies to compete on service as well.
4. Suppliers to Amazon have substantial bargaining power. The wholesalers are selling to other companies as well as to individual customers and some of the publishers are starting their own websites. Also, backward integration is much too expensive in this industry and the suppliers

(publisher) are each offering a different product (author/book), making it impossible to force competition of suppliers.

5 The threat of substitute products is high for the retail industry. In selling books, music and movies a substitute is to borrow from the library, rent from a store (videos) or download from the Internet (music).

In the case of Amazon.com, the five forces can be seen as threats because all five are strong. Porter argues that when the forces of competition are strong, the company has little ability to raise prices—therefore limiting profitability (see Figure B).

The external portion of the SWOT analysis is the Opportunities and Threats. Opportunities arise when a company can take advantage of a situation in the industry, and a threat is a situation where the company may have trouble adjusting the market.

Opportunities

■ Willingness of investors to contribute capital to dot-coms. With a bull market, largely due to baby boomers planning for retirement, a technology company could raise fast capital by issuing more shares of stock.

■ Bezos purposely started his company in Seattle because of the wealth of computer-minded people. Experienced programmers would be in abundance.

■ Buying on the Internet was easy and fast. Buyers are looking for a bargain and are using the latest technology. The economy was booming in 1998, too.

■ The ability to create their own software to do exactly what their customers want, as well as going the extra mile to offer services they didn't even know they wanted.

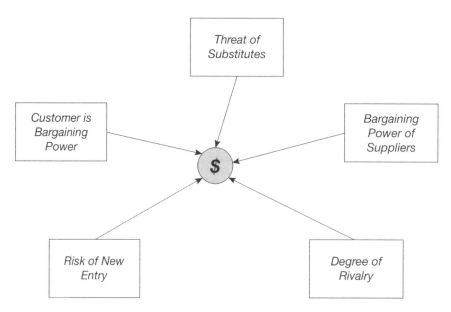

Figure B *Porter's Five Competitive Forces apply in pressure to profits.*

- The high boundaries to entry because of the investment in intelligence and software to manage the huge amount of orders and services.
- Ability to attract quality employees from other large companies.
- Attraction of their name to build affiliations with other websites.
- Computers are becoming as popular as televisions in homes. In turn, raising the popularity of the Internet, which equals more customers for the company.
- Globalization of the economy. The U.S. holds only a fraction of the world's population; expanding overseas dramatically increases customer base.
- New technology creating more profitable, downloadable products such as MP3s and ebooks.
- Real-time, online sales, purchasing and marketing data—that is the world of e-Commerce.
- The ability to order goods from the suppliers and have them shipped directly to the customer. This lowers costs of storing inventory and makes it possible to diversify and reach economies of scale.

Threats

- The low boundaries to entry because of the enormous amount of titles available to consumers and the low investment needed to start a ".com" company.
- One of the drawbacks of e-tailing is the cost of shipping. The cost is passed to the customer, raising the total cost of the item, but without adding any value. Due to the limited number of shipping companies, the e-tailer has little bargaining power over price.
- Brick and mortar bookstores expanding across the nation, around the globe, and soon taking their name recognition to the world wide web; as well as publishers, for example, Simon & Schuster (VIACOM.)
- Security is a major issue when doing business online. E-commerce companies must stay one step ahead of the hackers by implementing very expensive security solutions.
- The public has a negative attitude towards the "category killers." Have you ever seen "You've Got Mail?" People do not look favorably upon big businesses taking over small, local establishments.
- The Internet is headed in so many directions it is hard to predict any market.
- Barnes & Noble and Bertelsmann joining forces to offer books in several languages around the world.
- Still about half of the world is not "connected" to the Internet, limiting the marketplace.
- Non-price competition is expensive for Amazon because it is impossible to differentiate their books from their competitors. They must differentiate their services and at the same time lower their costs.

Internal Analysis

The Internal Analysis is going to identify the basis of competitive advantage for Amazon.com. Competitive advantage is the product of at least one of the following: superior efficiency, quality, innovation and customer responsiveness. When we look at the strengths of the company, we can see that Amazon.com has a good competitive advantage over companies in the same industry. Nevertheless, Amazon.com has weaknesses that could affect its performance in the near future if not addressed.

Strengths

- Amazon.com uses technology to offer services that a traditional store or catalog cannot match. Its users can access a database of 1.1 million titles without the hassle of finding call numbers or locating books on shelves. A customer can browse through a database five times superior to the largest super store's inventory and search by subject, favorite authors, or titles. When a book is selected, Amazon.com is programmed to display other related titles that the customer might find interesting. Amazon also informs customers about new upcoming books via electronic mail. This demonstrates superior innovation.

- Amazon has a well-built system on cross-selling products. By allowing viewers to post their own reviews of books they read, Amazon lets its customers sell to each other while maintaining confidentiality. Customers can also read book reviews by professionals, such as the *New York Times*. They can ask for recommendations or recommend books to others. This type of setting makes it very easy for two strangers to share ideas, which would otherwise be impossible.

- Amazon.com is strong on customer focus and involvement. They involve their customers in building sites, which guarantees customer satisfaction. The music store was designed with the help of more than 20,000 customers who responded to the invitation to build the music store of their dreams. Customers wanted a site with rich musical selection, great prices, features and customer service. Many of the new features in the new music store are the direct result of these suggestions.

- Amazon.com incorporates four core value propositions: Convenience, Selection, Service and Price. The reasons people give when asked why they shop at Amazon.com are that they are busy and it's convenient, or that they have a big selection, and they've been reliable.

- Amazon advertises aggressively and spends money marketing its services to increase name recognition, among other things. They have successfully splashed their name on the gateway of most sites on the web. The firm spent more than $340,000 in the first half of 1996 and was ranked thirty-fourth in web ad spending. Advertising has contributed greatly in the rapid growth of the Amazon Associates Program. Creating a referral service from other websites helped this program increase traffic to Amazon.com. They also placed linked advertisements on partners' websites to have the ability to track customers coming from these various sites.

- The firm is open for business twenty-four hours a day and has a global presence. This gives them a great advantage over traditional bookstores. More than 3 million customers from 160 countries have purchased books from the firm, also proving international success.

- Skilled and committed staff members exist at Amazon.com. Amazon has the asset of a very bright CEO (Jeff Bezos), as well as some of the brightest computer programmers in the country. Managers have high level of competence and intelligence and employees work hard, long and smart. In addition to that, employees act like owners because they are given stock options.

- Amazon.com is very much a consumer oriented and friendly website. They appreciate customer loyalty and strive to increase customer satisfaction. Ease of use and ability of customers to browse by author, subject and title is a quality they possess. Customer responsiveness is very good. Orders are processed immediately, and Amazon has a service where if a book is unavailable or out of print, a customer can place a request. Amazon will look for the book and post a wanted advertisement on their website.

- Amazon.com offers customers low prices. Almost all books are discounted. Bestsellers are sold at a 30 to 40 percent discount and the other books at a 10 percent discount. Since all sales are conducted online, Amazon has very low real estate costs and no store costs. By working effectively, they can reduce the price of their products.

Weaknesses

■ Amazon.com has a high reliance on Internet and e-mail services. Practically everything, up to 90 percent of customer service, is conducted through either e-mail or the Internet. Too much money is invested into building e-commerce solutions. A good example is the customer service e-mail center.

■ Competing with multiple categories and in different industries has also resulted in a weakness. Amazon.com has shown weak profit after adding its music stores. Unlike book retailers, many online music stores, such as cdnow.com, have been in operation for more than a few years. For example, cdnow.com claims that it is the world's leading online music store by offering more than 250,000 music-related items. Existing online music stores already have a large portion of music sales and are very competitive.

■ Amazon.com is also so much focused on its own growth and customer responsiveness that it might not see a competition rise up and overthrow the company. This is an example of the Icarus Paradox. Many companies become so dazzled by their early success that they believe more of the same type of effort is the way to future success. As a result, a company can lose sight of market realities and the fundamental requirement for achieving a competitive advantage.

■ Shipment waiting time could be seen as a weakness at Amazon.com. After placing an order, a customer has to wait a couple of days to receive those items. Unfortunately, if this is urgent, customers might prefer to buy items from local bookstores or borrow items from the library and get them in hours rather than days.

■ Amazon.com has a high cost of employment. Employees are experts in what they do and very dedicated to the growth and development of the company. Nevertheless they are highly paid, and one of the problems Amazon faces is this high cost of employment.

Knowledge Management

One of the competitive advantages of Amazon.com has been the quality of its people. The highly successful company goes to extraordinary lengths to hire people with strong intellects and capabilities. One reason for this is the fast-changing nature of the e-commerce industry in which it competes. Unlike many firms, its IT group does not tolerate "legacy people" whose skills have become obsolete. The knowledge base for Amazon.com IT must always be current. Therefore, the IT group has focused heavily on the issue of identifying and maintaining knowledge competencies.

Although no specific mention was made to how or if KM was used or implemented into Amazon.com, we have learned that KM is required in every formalized organization. To explain how KM might be used at Amazon we looked at another company similar to Amazon.com.

In this company they looked at the issue of knowledge competencies. Their goal was to create an online competency profile for jobs and employees within the corporation. The project was focused not on entry-level competencies, but rather on those needed and acquired to stay on the leading edge of the workplace. However, shortcomings in the educational system must be addressed by competencies acquired on the job.

The goal is to use the competency model to transfer and build knowledge, not merely to test it. When the organization's employees have a better idea of what competencies are required of them, they will be better consumers of educational offerings within and outside the company.

They first established base-level competencies, which became known as foundation knowledge. They were:

- foundation;
- local: unique competencies; advanced skills that apply to a particular job type;
- global: present in all employees within a particular function or organization; and
- universal: universal to all employees within company.

Within each of the four foundation competencies there are two different types. Explicit competencies involve knowledge of and experience with specific tools or methods. Implicit competencies involve more abstract thinking and reasoning. Explicit competencies change quite frequently while implicit competencies are expected to remain stable over time.

The most important Problem/Opportunity that we have come across is the continued saturation of the online book market. Due to the entry of Borders.com and Barnes & Noble.com, not to mention the ten new book retailers per month, we see a dimming future opportunities. Though Amazon.com owns the number one spot in book-retailing, diversifying is *strongly* recommended.

It has been proven that their customers will stick with them as they diversify. Here is our proof, Amazon.com's "music store," wherein customers could purchase CDs and cassettes from their favorite musicians became the number one online music retailer in one business quarter. This is an enormous accomplishment for the company and substantial proof that expansion is desired.

After the online music store opened, the online video store opened; in six weeks, Amazon became the number one online retailer of video. Amazon.com has built a strong online name. A name that people trust and look to for retail. We feel that with Amazon's current image it could become an online "Wal-Mart," offering an enormous array of products, all at the lowest price.

Although Amazon.com is still in the early stages of learning how to bring new value to its customers through Internet commerce and merchandising, its goal still remains the same, "to solidify and extend its brand and customer base." This requires sustained investment in systems and infrastructure to support outstanding customer convenience, selection and service while they grow. Although Amazon.com has established a strong leadership position, it is certain that competition will even further accelerate the challenges and hurdles Amazon.com will face in meeting their long-term objectives.

Case Exercise References

www.amazon.com.

www.bordersstore.com.

amazon.com.inc, *New York Times,* July 19, 2007.

Questions for Discussion

1 What are the key issues regarding KM in this case exercise?

2 What are the respective people/technology/process aspects of KM in this case exercise?

3 Do you think that Amazon effectively organizes its knowledge?

4 How is intelligence gathered?

FURTHER READING

Sveiby, K. (1997) The New Organizational Wealth: Managing and Measuring Intangible Assets. San Francisco: Berret Kochler Publishers.

Wickramasinghe, N. and von Lubitz, D. (2007) *Knowledge-based Enterprise Theories and Fundamentals*. Hershey, PA: IGI.

www.gurteen.com.

www.fek.su.se/home/bic/meritum/download/index.html#papers.

www.sveiby.com.

REFERENCES

Bali, R.K. and Dwivedi, A.N. (2004) Organizational Culture and the Implementation of Management Information Systems, *OR Insight*, 17(1): 10–18.

Brooking, A. (1996) *Intellectual Capital, Core Assets for the Third Millennium Enterprise*. London: International Thompson Business Press.

Danish Agency for Trade and Industry (2000) A Guideline for Intellectual Capital Statements—A Key to Knowledge Management. Available online at www.ebst.dk/publikationer/rapporter/guidelineICS/ren.htm (accessed July 25, 2008)

Dwivedi, A.N., Bali, R.K., Naguib, R.N.G., and Lehaney, B. (2005) Knowledge Management for the Healthcare Sector: Lessons from a Case Study, *OR Insight*, 18(2): 3–13.

Edvinsson, L. and Malone, M. (1997) *Intellectual Capital: Realizing Your Company's True Value by Finding Its Hidden Roots*. New York: Harper Business.

Kaplan, R. and Norton, D. (1996) *The Balanced Scorecard: Translating Strategy into Action*. Boston, MA: Harvard Business School Press.

Lehaney, B., Malindzak, D., and Khan, Z. (2008) Simulation Modeling for Problem Understanding: A Case Study in the East Slovakia Coal Industry. Accepted for publication in the *Journal of the Operational Research Society*.

Lehaney, B., Clarke, S., Coakes, E., and Jack, G. (2004) *Beyond Knowledge Management*. Hershey, PA: Idea Group Publishing.

Malhotra, Y. (2003) Measuring Knowledge Assets of a Nation: Knowledge Systems for Development, Research Paper presented to UN. Available online from http://unpan1.un.org/intradoc/groups/public/documents/un/unpan011601.pdf (accessed July 6, 2002).

Mehta, N. (2007) The Value Creation Cycle: Moving Towards a Framework for Knowledge Management Implementation, *Knowledge Management Research and Practice*, 5(2): 126–135.

MERITUM Project (2002) Guidelines for Managing and Reporting on Intangibles (Intellectual Capital Report). Available online at www.fek.su.se/home/bic/meritum/download/index.html#papers (accessed July 17, 2008).

Nonaka, I. and Takeuchi, H. (1995) *The Knowledge Creating Company: How Japanese Companies Create the Dynamics of Innovation.* New York: OUP.

Polanyi, M. (1962) *Personal Knowledge: Towards a Post-critical Philosophy.* New York: Harper Torchbooks.

Probst, G., Raub, S., and Romhardt, K. (2000) *Managing Knowledge: Building Blocks for Success.* Chichester: John Wiley & Sons.

Roos, G., Pike, S., and Ferntröm, L. (2005) *Managing Intellectual Capital in Practice.* Amsterdam: Elsevier.

Roos, J., Roos, G., Edvinsson, L., and Dragonetti, N. (1997) *Intellectual Capital: Navigating in the New Business Landscape.* New York: Macmillan.

Skyrme, D. and Amidon, D. (1997) *Creating the Knowledge-based Business.* London: Business Intelligence.

Skyrme, D. (2005) Measuring the Value of Knowledge. Available online at www.skyrme.com/insights/24kmeas.htm (accessed September 1, 2008).

Sveiby, K. (1997) The Intangible Assets Monitor, *Journal of Human Resource Costing and Accounting,* 2(1): 73–97.

Sveiby, K. (2006) Knowledge Management Initiatives Round the Globe. Available online at www.sveiby.com/KnowledgeManagementInitiativesRoundtheGlobe/tabid/123/Default.aspx (accessed July 28, 2008).

Chapter 3

Knowledge Tools and Techniques

INTRODUCTION

There are several different tools and techniques heavily used within KM. Some actively use technology, some less so or not at all. This chapter will introduce some of the major methods in contemporary use and will provide some examples to illustrate their effectiveness.

TAXONOMIES AND ONTOLOGIES

Ontologies and taxonomies are means of classifying things. This notion is not new, and the concept is often attributed to Aristotle (384 BC–322 BC), who attempted to classify living things (in ways that are still familiar today, such as live-birth animals (mammals) and egg-birth creatures (birds and fish)). The term taxonomy thus began to be used within biology and was used to classify living organisms (this is now known as alpha taxonomy). It is now used in a more general sense, and may refer to the ways in which classifications are decided, not just the classification structure itself. Interestingly, systems thinking also has biological roots and this is discussed in Chapter 4.

Ontologies are often considered as broader than taxonomies, but the terms may be used in a variety of ways. Various relationships can be classified and grandparent–parent–child relationships are often depicted. The term can, however, be used to cover multi-parent relationships and networks. For example, a document may be classified with the parent Bloggs (the author). It might also have the parent June 2008 (date) or the parent Tax Office (correspondent). It could be classified by subject.

A very well-known classification scheme is that used by libraries, known as the *Dewey Decimal Classification* (DDC) or the *Dewey Decimal System*, originally created by Melvil Dewey in 1876. Within DDC, knowledge is organized into ten main classes, ten divisions per class (100 divisions) and ten sections per division (1,000 sections)—hence decimal. Non-fiction publications are classified by subject as follows.

From the above, 600 represents technology, and within this the second digit indicates the division: 600 is used for general works on technology, 610 for medicine and health, 620 for

Table 3.1 *Example of the Dewey Decimal System*

000	Computer science, information, and general works
100	Philosophy and psychology
200	Religion
300	Social sciences
400	Language
500	Science
600	Technology
700	Arts and recreation
800	Literature
900	History, geography, and biography

engineering, 630 for agriculture, and so on. The third digit indicates the section with 610 used for general works on medicine and health, 611 for human anatomy, 612 for human physiology, and 613 for personal health and safety. After the first three digits a decimal point is used, followed by finer gradations, each being a factor of ten.

Just as an example, if you wanted to find out about black widow spiders of California, you would look for 595.44. Each book in a library will have its Dewey number on the spine. A major advantage of this system is that when books are left on desks or misplaced on shelves, it is extremely easy to put them back in the correct place, without having to start considering from the beginning where they should go.

The Dewey System is an example of a taxonomy that is used worldwide. It can make life easier, because as human beings we like to try and make sense of things by putting some order on them that we can understand. A problem with this is that one person's order and understanding is not the same as another's. The book *Who Moved My Cheese?* is a humorous view on change in personal and work life and nothing to do with culinary issues. Someone classifying the work might think otherwise—and so there are lots of rules about how to classify with Dewey so that the same book title would be classified in every library in exactly the same way.

A major problem with this is of course the cost of setting up all the rules, the training involved, the supervision, the checking, etc. The Dewey System has evolved over a long period of time, so this has not been the major challenge that it would be for a large organization suddenly deciding it wished to classify its knowledge.

The technology aspects of KM are largely derived from computer science, within which ontology represents a domain, the concepts within it, and the relationships between those concepts. In this sense an ontology would typically comprise a structure of individuals (e.g. a specific child), classes (e.g. all children with red hair), relationships between classes and individuals, attributes (e.g. age), constraints and rules, events (how things change—e.g. hair changes from red to grey), and various other factors, such as axioms and functions. Together these all comprise the domain.

KM may use taxonomy to depict an organization, and this may be done in different ways, such as by product, by customer type, by cost center, by services bought, and so on. The driver is knowledge transfer to achieve competitive advantage, but the costs and effort of setting up such a system may be prohibitive. Attempting to organize knowledge methodically is typically a major task that is outside normal productive work. There is no immediate contribution to income, and there will be costs. Information and new ideas would have to be recognized and collated from the broadest to the most detailed level.

For the immediate future the key areas of taxonomies in KM are likely to be in helping users to navigate web-pages and PDF files on a KM intranet, and in the construction of logs of experts in an organization. Taking eBay as an example, someone searching for a DVD player would find a taxonomy of this kind:

Home > Buy > Consumer Electronics > DVD & Home Cinema > DVD Players

This can be divided further by price band, manufacturer, region code, etc.

DATA MINING TOOLS AND TECHNIQUES

Due to the immense size of the data sets, computerized techniques are essential to help decision makers understand relationships and associations between data elements. Data mining is closely associated with databases and shares some common ground with statistics since both strive toward discovering structure in data. However, while statistical analysis starts with some kind of hypothesis about the data, data mining does not. Furthermore, data mining is much more suited to dealing with heterogeneous databases, data sets and data fields.

From a micro perspective, data mining is a vital step in the broader context of the knowledge discovery in databases (KDD) that transforms data into knowledge by identifying valid, novel, potentially useful, and ultimately understandable patterns in data (Adriaans and Zantinge, 1996; Fayyad et al., 1996; Cabena et al., 1998; Bendoly, 2003). KDD plays an important role in data-driven decision support systems that include query tools, report generators, statistical analysis tools, data warehousing and online analytic processing (OLAP). Data mining algorithms are used on data sets for model building, or for finding patterns and relationships in data. How to manage such newly discovered knowledge, as well as other organizational knowledge assets, is the realm of KM.

STEPS IN DATA MINING

The following steps are typically undertaken in data mining (Fayyad et al., 1996; Becerra-Fernandez and Sabherwal, 2001; Holsapple and Joshi, 2002; Choi and Lee, 2003). These steps are iterative, with the process moving backward whenever it is required to do so.

1   Develop an understanding of the application, of the relevant prior knowledge, and of the end user's goals.
2   Create a target data set to be used for discovery.
3   Clean and pre-process the data (including handling missing data fields, noise in the data, accounting for time series, and known changes).

4 Reduce the number of variables and find invariant representations of the data if possible.

5 Choose the data-mining task (classification, regression, clustering, etc.).

6 Choose the data-mining algorithm. — preces by a computer

7 Search for patterns of interest (this is the actual data mining).

8 Interpret the patterns mined. If necessary, iterate through any of steps 1–7.

9 Consolidate the knowledge discovered, prepare reports and then use/re-use the newly created knowledge.

A data mining project usually starts with data collection or data selection, covering almost all steps (described above) in the KDD process. In this respect, the first three steps of the KDD process (i.e. selection, pre-processing and transformation) are considered exploratory data mining, whereas the last two steps (i.e. data mining and interpretation/evaluation) in the KDD process are considered predictive data mining.

The primary objectives of data mining in practice tend to be description (performed by exploratory data mining) and prediction (performed by predictive data mining). Description focuses on finding human-interpretable patterns describing the data, while prediction involves using some observations and attributes to predict unknown or future values of other attributes of interest. The relative importance of description and prediction for particular data mining applications can vary considerably. The descriptive and predictive tasks are carried out by applying different machine learning, artificial intelligence and statistical algorithms.

Major goals of exploratory data mining are data cleaning, unification and understanding. Some of the data operations undertaken during exploratory data mining include: sampling, partitioning, charting, graphing, associating, clustering, transforming, filtering and imputing. Predictive data mining deals with future values of variables and utilizes many algorithms; including regression, decision trees and neural networks. Predictive data mining also involves an assessment step, which compares the effectiveness of different models according to many performance metrics.

Figure 3.1 shows an integrated view of the knowledge discovery process, the evolution of knowledge from data to information to knowledge, and the types of data mining (exploratory and predictive) and their interrelationships. In this one figure, all the major aspects connected with data mining are captured, emphasizing its integral role in knowledge creation. This is not normally explicitly articulated in the existing literature although the connection between data, information and knowledge is often discussed (Chung and Gray, 1996; Becerra-Fernandez and Sabherwal, 2001; Holsapple and Joshi, 2002; Choi and Lee, 2003).

Data mining then, is the non-trivial process of identifying valid, novel, potentially useful, and ultimately understandable patterns from data (Fayyad et al., 1996). It is essential to emphasize here the importance of the interaction with experts who always play a crucial and indispensable role in any knowledge discovery process in facilitating prediction of key patterns and also identification of new patterns and trends.

BUSINESS INTELLIGENCE AND ANALYTICS

Business intelligence (BI) has now become synonymous with an umbrella description for a wide range of decision-support tools, some of which target specific user audiences

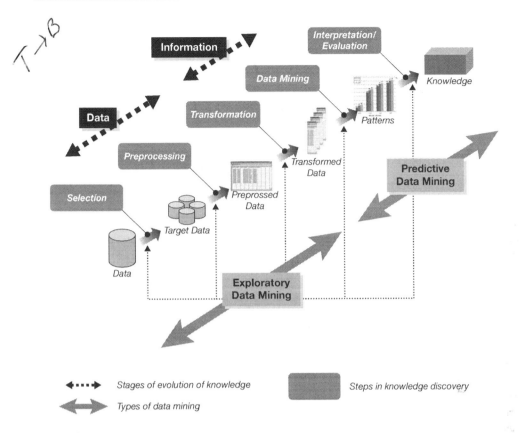

T→B

Figure 3.1 *Essential Aspects of Data Mining.*
Source: adapted from Fayyad *et al.* (1996)

(Wickramasinghe, 2006; Wickramasinghe and Schaffer, 2006). At the bottom of the BI hierarchy are extraction and formatting tools, which are also known as data-extraction tools. These tools collect data from existing databases for inclusion in data warehouses and data marts. Thus the next level of the BI hierarchy is known as warehouses and marts.

Because the data come from so many different, often incompatible systems in various file formats, the next step in the BI hierarchy is formatting tools; these tools and techniques are used to "cleanse" the data and convert it into formats that can easily be understood in the data warehouse or data mart. Next, tools are needed to support the reporting and analytical techniques. These are known as enterprise reporting and analytical tools. OLAP (online analytic process) engines and analytical application-development tools are for professionals who analyze data, for example, by forecasting, modeling and trend analysis. Human intelligence tools form the next level in the hierarchy and involve human expertise, opinions and observations to be recorded to create a knowledge repository.

These tools are at the very top of the BI hierarchy and serve to amalgamate analytical and BI capabilities along with human expertise. Business analytics (BA) is a newer term that tends to be viewed as a sub-set of the broader business intelligence umbrella and concentrates on the analytic aspects within BI by focusing on the simultaneous analysis of patterns and trends in a given context (Wickramasinghe and Schaffer, 2006).

COMMUNITIES OF PRACTICE

The term "Communities of Practice" (CoP) is largely attributed to the work of Wenger (1998). The term refers to a network of people, working on the same or similar areas, coming together (either physically or virtually) to share and develop their collective knowledge. The intention is that this would benefit them as individuals as well as the organization.

By way of example, a CoP might be working in the area of healthcare modeling, and, more specifically, might be attempting to provide decision support tools in order to make better use of resources. Aspects of CoPs include communal support, social learning and shared culture. As with all organizational culture, it can be learnt by new entrants. In relatively recent times, CoPs have been considered in the context of KM, and they relate to developing social capital and sharing tacit knowledge. While a lot of KM initiatives are intra-organizational, CoPs may be intra-organizational, inter-organizational or a mix of both. They may even be trans-national.

The notion of CoPs incorporates learning as a major focal issue, and this relates strongly to organizational learning and learning organizations (discussed later in this book). Learning is generally a social activity and therefore participation and its nature within social communities is of importance in CoPs. Engagement in CoPs may be viewed as a way in which the individual helps establish his or her own identity and this identity relates to processes of change.

Change management, therefore, is an interesting link, but change management is normally considered as a concept that is used within an organization. Without an organizational structure and without effective line management, lots of complex questions arise, such as who decides what changes should be made, how should they be made, what are their benefits and cost, how are these measured, who decides and negotiates meaning, and who manages all of this?

CoPs may be within a subject discipline, or they may be within an application area that involves people from a variety of subject disciplines. The latter may enable more holistic approaches to be taken to viewing areas of interest, and it also adds to the richness of perspective while offering theoretical triangulation. This is about looking at something from different theoretical perspectives. If there is convergence of views, it provides stronger credibility than would be gained from a single theoretical view, as the latter might have a particular bias.

The learning aspect of CoPs is inherent within the concept of organizational learning. It is about how flexible an organization may be and how easily it can adapt to new situations that reflect changes in the internal and external environments.

Within the business world, CoPs are now considered to be much more than merely sharing day-to-day practices within the community. Wenger explains practice as *meaning*—an experience that is of interest located in a process referred to as the *negotiation of meaning*. This negotiation requires active *participation*, defined as:

> . . . the social experience of living in the world in terms of membership in social communities and active involvement in social enterprises . . . it can involve all kinds of relations, conflictual as well as harmonious, intimate as well as political, competitive as well as cooperative.
>
> (Wenger, 1998: 55–56)

A schematic may help to explain the concepts. Figure 3.2 depicts the "KARMAH Starwheel," a representation of a CoP created and facilitated by the KM for Healthcare (KARMAH)

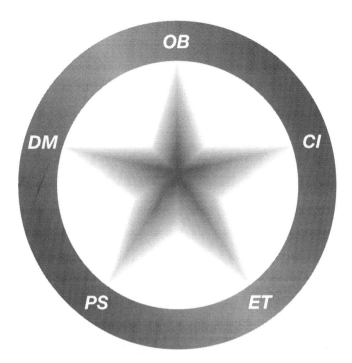

Figure 3.2 *KARMAH "Starwheel".*
www.coventry.ac.uk/karmah/—reproduced with permission

research group at Coventry University, U.K. Essentially, as the group's interests match those of KM within the healthcare environ, the span of knowledge is widespread, depicted by five distinct avenues (expanded in Table 3.2).

At the time of writing, participation in KARMAH's CoP is by invitation only. Having recognized that the nature of Healthcare KM is such that a blend of key skills is required to achieve true progress in this rapidly evolving area, the "Starwheel" depicts the group's strategy for efficient sharing and debate of current knowledge in the field. The schematic shows how

Table 3.2 *The KARMAH Research Group's Spread of Competencies*

OB	Organizational Behavior including change management, strategy, ICTs, clinical governance, etc.
CI	Clinical Informatics and Engineering including AI, cybernetics, expert systems, etc.
ET	Education and Training including HRM, work study, industry-academic interfaces, etc.
PS	Privacy and Security including technical, legal, ethical and organizational aspects, etc.
DM	Data Mining including algorithms, knowledge discovery, genomic mining, etc.

participants, with expertise and competencies in the given areas (e.g. OB, CI, etc.) can bring key ideas to a central repository (the center of the star), from which other members can draw/amend/add before returning back to the center for final refinement. At the same time, members are free to interact by moving directly across the wheel. In this manner, it is envisaged that this will lead to an increased and rapid level of publication and/or collaborative projects for all active participants. This is a useful example of a multidisciplinary CoP.

STORYTELLING AND THE POWER OF NARRATIVE

The Girl and the Frog

A five year old girl was playing in the garden early one evening while her parents and her parents' friends chatted and sipped Martinis on the deck. After a few minutes, the girl walked to her parents, with her hands gently clasped, and showed them her new friend: a frog. "I'm going to call him Freddy—Freddy the Frog" she said.

The parents duly complimented her and Freddy. Perhaps startled by all of the attention, Freddy leapt out of the girl's hands and jumped into a hole. The girl screamed for the grown-ups to rescue Freddy. Their adult responsibility perhaps fuelled by their drinks, the grown-ups attempted to retrieve the frog. They tried to reach him with their hands and arms but Freddy was out of reach.

They then thought of placing a long stick in the hole, perhaps in the vain hope that Freddy, grateful for the support, would clutch the stick and be rescued. Sadly, the slightly drunk adults only succeeded in occasionally poking the frog with the stick. "You're hurting him!" cried the girl. "Stop it!"

After a few minutes, despite the girl's protests, the adults gave up. After attempting to comfort the crying girl, they returned to the deck and their conversation. Five minutes later, the girl joined them on the deck, her hands again gently clasped around Freddy. "How did you get him out?" the puzzled adults asked.

The girl smiled. "Oh, I just filled the hole with water."

HAVE YOU HEARD THE ONE ABOUT . . . ?

The power and efficacy of narrative in the workplace has been well documented (Polkinghorne, 1988; Clandinin and Connelly, 2000). The use of effective narrative attempts to understand behavior by way of collections of anecdotal material. Narrative can be defined as a method that uses a variety of different data-based sources (for example, journals, notes, letters, transcribed conversations and discussions, interviews, photographs, etc.). The experience behind these items is of importance. It can be argued that narrative is closely related to qualitative research; they both share the trait of human knowledge.

Effective narrative should be finite and possess a longitudinal time sequence (i.e. it should have a beginning, a middle and an end). As Greenhalgh and Hurwitz (1999: 48) say, narrative:

Table 3.3 *Difference Between Story and Narrative*

Story	the telling of a happening or connected series of happenings, whether true or fictitious; account; narration.
Narrative	the broadest sense is: anything told or recounted; more narrowly, something told or recounted in the form of a story; account; tale.

. . . should also presuppose both a narrator and a listener whose different viewpoints affect how the story is told. Third, the narrative is concerned with individuals; rather than simply reporting what they do or what is done to them it concerns how those individuals feel and how people feel about them.

There is much academic debate over the exact distinction between the terms "narrative" and story. It is beyond the remit of this book to become embroiled in such a complex argument. We would, however, agree with Denning (2004) perspective (Table 3.3).

Storytelling can be a very useful and powerful communication tool, offering several advantages over more conventional mechanisms. These include Weaver (2005) who says that:

Stories communicate ideas holistically, conveying a rich yet clear message, and so they are an excellent way of communicating complicated ideas and concepts in an easy-to-understand form. Stories therefore allow people to convey tacit knowledge that might otherwise be difficult to articulate; in addition, because stories are told with feeling, they can allow people to communicate more than they realize they know.

Storytelling provides the context in which knowledge arises as well as the knowledge itself, and hence can increase the likelihood of accurate and meaningful knowledge transfer.

Stories are an excellent vehicle for learning, as true learning requires interest, which abstract principles and impersonal procedures rarely provide.

Stories are memorable—their messages tend to 'stick' and they get passed on.

Stories can provide a 'living, breathing' example of how to do something and why it works rather than telling people what to do, hence people are more open to their lessons.

Stories therefore often lead to direct action—they can help to close the "knowing-doing gap" (the difference between knowing how to do something and actually doing it).

Storytelling can help to make organizational communication more "human"—not only do they use natural day-to-day language, but they also elicit an emotional response as well as thoughts and actions.

Stories can nurture a sense of community and help to build relationships.

People enjoy sharing stories—stories enliven and entertain.

The more interesting and powerful the tale, the more one is likely to remember it. Whether or not this makes it more useful in the workplace is a different matter. By way of example, the following is an example of a powerful hospital-based tale.

The Patient's Eye

A man ran into the Accident and Emergency department of his local hospital. In obvious pain, he clutched his right eye which was swollen to almost three times its normal size. Tears streaming down his eyes, he managed to convince the reception nurse of his urgent need. He told the doctor that his contact lens had somehow "fused" to his eyeball. "I was taking out my contacts and one is stuck on my eyeball! Help me, please!"

The doctor was horrified but, after careful examination of the eye, could find nothing obviously wrong (apart from the immense swelling). The patient howled in pain, all the while attempting to itch and scratch his eye. "My eye!" he cried. "For God's sake, fix my eye!"

The doctor called two of his senior colleagues who rushed the now hysterical patient to a lab. After administering a pain-killing injection (which helped somewhat to calm the patient down), all manner of additional lighting and laser-based medical equipment was wheeled in to analyze the patient's eye. After several minutes, the doctors had drawn a blank. They scratched their heads and looked at each other.

One doctor suddenly had a thought. "Actually . . . are you absolutely sure you hadn't already removed the lens?"

The full impact of this option dawned on everyone in the lab. What the patient had in fact tried to do was to "peel" away part of his cornea.

We fully acknowledge that this story is particularly graphic. However, once we look past this, what—if anything—have we actually learnt? To be careful? To be sure? What organizational implications are there? If we adapt the story though so that the doctor who, at the end of the story, had the idea now appears as a junior doctor, or perhaps an attending nurse or auxiliary, the story suddenly has implications for practice within the hospital. The ability to examine all options, no matter where they come from, becomes very important. The experienced doctors examined the patient using all manner of expensive medical equipment and were unable to come to a diagnosis. The answer came from an unexpected source. There are potential lessons here, including the ability to consider all possible options. The simplest may be correct.

The power of storytelling (and a good narrative) boils down to accessibility. No technical knowledge per se is required. Any organizational member can understand a good tale. As understanding of the "meaning behind the tale" is grasped, this may lead to members sharing their own anecdotes and experiences. In this way, members can learn from each other.

SOCIAL NETWORKS (AND SOCIAL NETWORKING SITES)

In its simplest form, a social network is a structure comprised of several nodes (entities which could be companies, institutions or people) that are interconnected according to varying dependencies and interdependencies (Figure 3.3). These could include common interest, value, linkages and so forth. Given the myriad of different possibilities, the resulting visualization can be very complex (see Figure 3.3). Social Network Analysis (SNA) examines these relationships as linkages (ties) between nodes (the actors within the network). The social

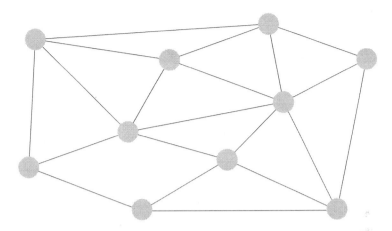

Figure 3.3 *Simple Social Network.*

networks (and contacts) combine to form *social capital*, considered to be of vital importance for communities and individuals (Putnam *et al.*, 2000).

The fact that relationships matter is a key concept within social capital theory (Field, 2003). As interactions allow people to create communities and a sense of belonging, the rich experience of a trustworthy social network can produce great advantages to the individuals within the social network. The "trustworthiness" of the network is essential as trust between individuals (known persons within the network) has broader implications for people outside the network (strangers) with whom interactions (face-to-face) would eventually take place (Beem, 1999). Without this essential interaction, trust breaks down, causing major social problems.

SOCIAL NETWORKING (INTERNET-BASED)

The proliferation of web-based social networking includes recent phenomena such as wikis, blogging, chat, instant messaging, file sharing, file exchange, video and contact management. The "social" aspect (the ability for individual users within the trustworthy environment to "tag" important documents and items—thus saving valuable time for other interested users) has key advantages for contemporary organizations. When this is combined with opinion and fact-finding from individuals, these comment-based contributions can combine to provide the basis for a useful CoP.

INTELLECTUAL CAPITAL

Intellectual capital is essentially knowledge that can be exploited for financial purposes. It combines knowledge present in the minds of individuals with the more traditional (and economic) aspect of capital. The knowledge can be both tacit and explicit. Due to the inherent nature and importance of *trust*, explained earlier in this chapter, it is implicit that intellectual capital also contains social capital.

KNOWLEDGE ASSETS

Knowledge assets refer to knowledge of products, services, processes, technologies, competitors and so forth that organizations require to gain and to maintain competitive edge and adapt to changing circumstances. The inherent issue remains the fact that such knowledge is always nearly "intangible," thus making it difficult to codify. Knowledge resides in the minds of individuals and the teams in which they function and therefore both teams and individuals have value for an organization which may be measured.

KNOWLEDGE NUGGETS

A knowledge nugget is a small item or piece of useful knowledge in categories of interest to the user. Sometimes the nugget can consist of relevant files, hyperlinks or dialogue boxes. In the contemporary web-enabled environment, nuggets can include external links to wikis, podcasts and videocasts.

CONCLUSIONS

There are key tools and techniques closely related to contemporary KM (in addition to those which evolve), several of which have been outlined in this chapter. Some of these techniques utilize IT but all rely on an effective human component to both enliven and enable them.

SUMMARY

Key KM-related tools and techniques have been outlined. These include taxonomies and ontologies (the Dewey Decimal System being a prime example), data mining, business intelligence and analytics, CoPs, the usefulness of storytelling and the power of narrative, social networks (with the growth of social networking sites being of contemporary relevance), intellectual capital, knowledge assets and knowledge nuggets.

REVIEW QUESTIONS

1 What are contemporary KM-related tools and techniques?

2 What is data mining?

3 What is storytelling?

4 What is social networking?

DISCUSSION QUESTIONS

1 How may data mining be used to create useful knowledge?

2 Why can CoPs be so useful?

3 Can data mining be carried out without human involvement?

4 How may storytelling and narrative be used to collect and analyze *tacit* knowledge?

CASE EXERCISE: FUJITSU UK[3]

Fujitsu is the third largest IT company in the world. Its headquarters are in Japan and it has large divisions in the U.K. and the U.S. It deals with different types of industries, including financial services, retail, government, healthcare and utilities. It is a company that spans markets, which include computing products, telecommunications, microelectronics and IT services.

One of the IT services is consulting, and Fujitsu UK provides a KM consulting service. This is something they take very seriously and they treat it as more than just a trend or a fad.

Knowledge Management Ideologies

Fujitsu UK has an interesting philosophy to KM that many of the other companies do not take into consideration. At Fujitsu UK, it is believed that a KMS should have two areas of concern. There should be a global strategy, and local implementation (Brompton). This means that there should be organizational benefits realized that will affect the company as a whole, but it must be fitted to different aspects of the organization.

This makes for a hybrid of the top-down and bottom-up approaches. This is Fujitsu UK's main theory when it comes to KM. They believe that a successful KMS requires both of these strategies. This seems like a good idea in theory, but from certain cases it seems to be hard enough for a company to implement one of these strategies, let alone a combination of the two.

Dupont had a system that was rather unstructured and complicated because of the fact that there was little support of the system from top management. This made it difficult to utilize the system for benefiting the organization as a whole. The lack of guidance from top management also could have made lower management and employees question the relevance and usefulness of the system.

Fujitsu UK might say that the first thing Dupont should have done was to get top management behind a KMS and decide how they wanted it to benefit the company. This would set strategies and assess long-term goals, and would put the top-down structure into effect. Then they would have Dupont do what they did in the case with respect to establishing the freedom of the bottom-up structure. The bottom-up is a good structure for an R&D firm, but it has little chance of succeeding without support from the top. There were other issues with Dupont, but this is just one aspect of how Fujitsu UK's main theories could have affected them.

The hybrid theory seems to be an ideal. Whether or not it is ideal in the terms that it seems to be the best, but it cannot be attained, or it is the best because it must be obtained, is the dilemma. But one would have to imagine that if a KMS does not have support from both the people who are going to fund and guide it, and from the people who are going to actually use the system, it will not reach its full potential and will eventually fade out.

Knowledge Management Approach

Fujitsu has many ideas about how KM can be effective to an organization and a few of these ideas will now be discussed.

The way Fujitsu UK approaches KM is focused on how the knowledge should be used. This deals with transferring the knowledge to the point of performance. This is just a fancy term for using the knowledge to get a specific task done. Where the knowledge is used to perform a task is the "point of performance."

They also stress the importance of the knowledge cycle. However, they do not do a good job at explaining why they stress this importance. The way the knowledge cycle is illustrated (see Figure D on p. 53), it shows the evolution of the cycle until it hits the "use" dimension. Then it continues around again. This is not explained by Fujitsu UK as to how to interpret this, but it can be assumed that knowledge should be used and reused, and it also could go through the cycle again to improve or enhance existing knowledge.

The type of knowledge that Fujitsu UK believes is the most important is transferable knowledge. This type of knowledge can be used right at the point of performance, without additional reflection, analysis or consolidation (Smith). This kind of knowledge is an ideal that is hard to obtain because almost any kind of knowledge probably has to be reflected on at some level, or even analyzed, so that it may be used effectively for a particular situation. Totally transferable knowledge is an absolute, an algorithm even, and probably will not be obtained very often.

Fujitsu UK notes that there are four dimensions of using knowledge that need to be taken into consideration. These dimensions are people, processes, organization and technology.

The people aspect deals with the importance of knowledge sharing, and motivation for using the knowledge system. This is one of the most important dimensions because the system is useless without this dimension. The process dimension deals with knowledge capture, knowledge filtering, and the expulsion of knowledge that is out of date. Organization is the other most important dimension because this lays out roles and policies of how knowledge will be dealt with. This supports Fujitsu UK's idea that the use of knowledge is the most important aspect of KM. The technology dimension lays out the means by which knowledge will be transferred to the point of performance, and the physical setup of the KMS.

Main KM Uses and Aids

One important use of KM to Fujitsu UK is in Value Management. This is essentially making business decisions by being better informed. This is especially helpful in the area of investing:

> Through initial engagements, we assess your business imperatives and desires and make recommendations based on real-world experience and client scenarios.
>
> (Strategic Consulting Service From Fujitsu)

By managing the knowledge gained from "real-world experience and client scenarios," Fujitsu UK helps companies make better business decisions.

Fujitsu UK also realizes that e-learning is a significant contributor to KM. This means that knowledge which is attainable by either collaboration with experts and other team members via e-mail, e-forums or telecommunication in general, can enhance the knowledge of an organization. This is a quicker and more effective way to learn about knowledge or create and capture knowledge in the organization because it is more accessible to people in the organization. It can be done anywhere in the world at any time.

Fujitsu UK vs Other Consulting Firms

When Fujitsu UK is compared to some of the other consulting firms, it tends to stand out as being ahead of the game. Of course, this probably has to do with the fact that the other cases are from the 1980s and 1990s, and the information from Fujitsu UK is current. Nevertheless, Fujitsu UK measures up as follows.

With the KM consulting service, Fujitsu UK deals with the consulting industry. It has been established that this particular industry was extremely competitive at those times and is more than likely even more competitive today.

The technology strategy for KPMG was to constantly be on the bleeding edge of technology, so as to have the best support for an evolving KMS. Fujitsu UK believes that too heavy an emphasis on technology can overshadow the importance of how the KMS will be used to benefit the organization. Being an IT company, Fujitsu UK obviously recognizes the importance of technology, but feels that it should not take precedence over knowledge use when developing and evolving a KMS.

A sharing culture is a staple at Andersen Consulting, but was severely lacking at KPMG. This is why KPMG was having problems with their KMS with respect to how it was not being used effectively. What good is a KMS if nobody will share knowledge through it? Fujitsu UK realizes the importance of a sharing culture and that the lack of one is one of the biggest impediments to a successful KMS.

KPMG had the most top-down structure of the consulting firms that have been discussed here, and the most linear structure for their KMS. This was proven to be ineffective because a heavy top-down structure "forces" knowledge sharing and the KMS onto lower divisions of the firm, and resistance to KM is more likely to be a problem. A linear approach to KM is also detrimental because there would be little tolerance to market or industry inconsistencies.

Fujitsu UK Case Studies

As discussed before, Fujitsu UK believes in a hybrid top-down/bottom-up approach because this will have top management support and lower level user support. Both are needed in some degree for a successful KMS. Fujitsu UK also believes that the idea of KM should be flexible. An attempt to demonstrate this is done by presenting cases that deal with how Fujitsu UK tries to implement KM into organizations in very different industries.

Fujitsu UK implemented a KMS for the UK Department of Health. The Department of Health realized that there was an enormous amount of knowledge floating around the organization and it needed to take action to organize and utilize that knowledge to make for an even better health department. In summary, Fujitsu UK helped the department create a top-down framework and build it upon the bottom-up framework of "knowledge sharing initiatives" that Fujitsu UK created earlier:

> Fujitsu has created a framework for a top-down strategic approach to ensure that KM and organizational strategy are aligned.
>
> (Department of Health)

Fujitsu UK also helped out the UK Court Service in a big way. The Court Service wanted jurors to be more knowledgeable about the court system before coming to jury duty. This would help jurors to be more focused on the case itself rather than being concerned about the whirlwind of the justice system that they have never had to deal with before. Fujitsu UK developed "Juror Online," which gives the juror a virtual tour of the UK justice system. A juror who is knowledgeable about the justice system can possibly make better decisions when it comes to the deliberation process.

The only thing wrong with this is that it is not KM. This is only letting jurors know what to expect when they come for duty, and that is all. If a juror wanted to do this, he could go and observe in his local court. The only thing different here is that it is more accessible because it is online. It is not to say that this is a bad idea, but it is not KM, and it seems like Fujitsu is trying to make it seem like it is. This could be a sign that Fujitsu UK might have KM confused with just simply providing information.

Questions and Criticisms

The key questions and criticisms of Fujitsu UK deal with exactly how flexible its idea of KM is to different industries. It tried to demonstrate this by giving access to various case studies, but it failed to provide different cases that dealt with KM. This leads to another point.

It seems like Fujitsu UK does a pretty good job with separating knowledge from information and data in theory, but the cases that it presents as KM cases are questionable as to the relevance of KM. There is one case in particular that mainly deals with information management and databases. It has little to no mention of knowledge or KM. Is this because Fujitsu UK is confusing information with knowledge? Their theories would lead one to believe they do not have a problem with this, but the way they present KM cases would say otherwise.

Conclusions and Lessons

Over all, Fujitsu UK seems like they would implement KM systems when they do actual KM consulting, and not organizational memory systems. This can be said because they harp on transferring knowledge to the point of performance. Their main point is that when companies want to implement KM, too many of them focus on capturing knowledge and technology first rather than on the kind of knowledge that would be needed and how it would be used for long-term benefits.

Fujitsu UK realizes that the knowledge transfer aspect is crucial, and this is what separates a KMS from an OMS. It would be beneficial for them, however, to always keep knowledge systems and information systems separated in order for their practices to reflect their theories. This lesson has been discussed time and time again in class, especially with the World Bank case. Mixing information into a KMS will make for a confusing and ineffective system.

Appendix

The Point of Performance illustration demonstrates the importance of the worker being in the middle because they will need access to all of the surrounding knowledge.

The Knowledge Cycle illustration can be a little confusing, especially since the word "us" in the box to the very right of the woman at the computer should be "use." It makes so much more sense

Figure C *KM approach supported with NEET.*

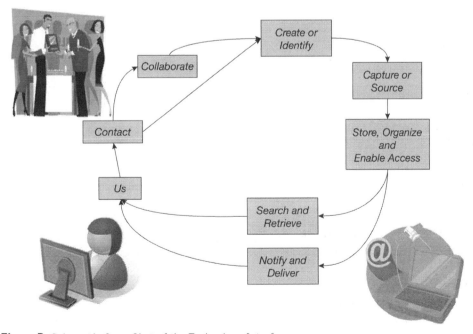

Figure D *Schematic Snap Shot of the Technology Interface.*

once that is realized. Fujitsu UK suggests reading this by starting at the "use" point, and going counter clockwise to make the point that before knowledge is even captured and stored, it should be assessed as to what kind of knowledge will be needed and how will it be used.

Case Exercise References

uk.fujitsu.com.

Smith, Mick, Transferring Knowledge to the Point of Performance, pdf available at uk.fujitsu.com.

Brompton, Allen (2002) Making Knowledge Management Work in Diverse and Autonomous Organizations, *Spectra Magazine*, Autumn edition. Available at: uk.fujitsu.com/services/consulting/knowledgemanagement/article_ spectra/uk.fujitsu.com/servicesproducts/casestudies/dept_health/ , Department of Health uk.fujitsu.com/services/ consulting/valuemanagement/ , Strategic Consulting Services from Fujitsu.

Case Exercise Questions

1   What are the key issues regarding KM in this case exercise?

2   Identify the respective people/technology/process aspects of KM in this case exercise?

3   What should be done next?

4   What are the major lessons learnt from this case exercise?

FURTHER READING

Wenger, E. (1998) *Communities of Practice: Learning, Meaning, and Identity*. Cambridge: Cambridge University Press.

Wickramasinghe, N. (2006) Knowledge Creation: A Meta-Framework, *International Journal of Innovation and Learning*, 3(5): 558–573.

REFERENCES

Adriaans, P. and Zantinge, D. (1996) *Data Mining*. Reading, MA: Addison-Wesley.

Becerra-Fernandez, I. and Sabherwal, R. (2001) Organizational Knowledge Management: A Contingency Perspective, *Journal of Management Information Systems*, 18(1), Summer: 23–55.

Beem, C. (1999) *The Necessity of Politics. Reclaiming American Public Life*. Chicago, IL: University of Chicago Press.

Bendoly, E. (2003) Theory and Support for Process Frameworks of Knowledge Discovery and Data Mining from ERP Systems, *Information & Management*, 40: 639–647.

Cabena, P., Hadjinian, P., Stadler, R., Verhees, J., and Zanasi, A. (1998) *Discovering Data Mining from Concept to Implementation*. Upper Saddle River, NJ: Prentice-Hall.

Choi, B. and Lee, H. (2003) An Empirical Investigation of KM Styles and Their Effect on Corporate Performance, *Information & Management*, 40: 403–417.

Chung, M. and Gray, P. (1996) Special Section: Data Mining, *Journal of Management Information Systems*, 16(1), Summer 1999: 11–16.

Clandinin, D.J. and Connelly, F.M. (2000) *Narrative Inquiry: Experience and Story in Qualitative Research*. San Francisco, CA: Jossey-Bass Publishers.

Denning, S. (2004) What Are the Main Types of Stories and Narratives? Available from www.stevedenning.com/Main_types_story.html (accessed 27 January 2009).

Fayyad, U., Piatetsky-Shapiro, G., and Smyth, P. (1996) From Data Mining to Knowledge Discovery: An Overview, in U. Fayyad, G. Piatetsky-Shapiro, P. Smyth, and R. Uthurusamy (Eds), *Advances in Knowledge Discovery and Data Mining*. Menlo Park, CA: AAAI Press/MIT Press.

Field, J. (2003) *Social Capital*. London: Routledge.

Greenhalgh, T. and Hurwitz, B. (1999) Narrative Based Medicine: Why Study Narrative?, *British Medical Journal*, 318: 48–50.

Holsapple, C. and Joshi, K. (2002) Knowledge Manipulation Activities: Results of a Delphi Study, *Information & Management*, 39: 477–519.

Polkinghorne, D. (1988) *Narrative Knowing and the Human Sciences*. Albany, NY: SUNY Press.

Putnam, R.D., Feldstein, L.M., and Cohen, D. (2000) *Bowling Alone: The Collapse and Revival of American Community*. New York: Simon & Schuster.

Weaver, C. (2005) *Storytelling*. Knowledge Management Specialist Library. Available online at www.library.nhs.uk/knowledgemanagement/ViewResource.aspx?resID=93580 (accessed May 29, 2008).

Wenger, E. (1998) *Communities of Practice: Learning, Meaning, and Identity*. Cambridge: Cambridge University Press.

Wickramasinghe, N. (2006) Knowledge Creation: A Meta-Framework, *International Journal of Innovation and Learning*, 3(5): 558–573.

Wickramasinghe, N. and Schaffer, J. (2006) Creating Knowledge Driven Healthcare Processes with the Intelligence Continuum, *International Journal of Electronic Healthcare*, 2(2): 164–174.

Chapter 4

Knowledge Management: A Systems View

INTRODUCTION

This chapter provides a background to systems thinking and develops arguments as to why and how systems thinking can relate strongly to KM. Successful KM requires the tools of operational research (OR) that assist managers to forecast, manage, monitor and plan; yet managers have often ignored the methodologies provided (Lehaney *et al.*, 1994). The reasons for this are manifold, and there has been a great deal of argument as to why, in practice, greater use is not made of modeling methodologies.

One view is that relatively "hard," prescriptive, goal seeking or optimizing methods have been perceived to fail. Problem structuring methodologies were developed within the concept of soft systems thinking, partly as an attempt to address this perceived failure by focusing on process issues. Later, critical systems thinking was developed as an approach that attempted to widen the issues and consider choice critically. These developments are related to systems thinking in general and will be discussed in more detail later in this chapter.

Essential features of systems thinking include the legitimacy of holism as opposed to reductionism. Reductionism may be considered as the process of simplifying the complex to define a specific experiment and providing a minimum explanation and analysis of problems, component by component. Within the concept of reductionism the whole is nothing more than the sum of its parts. Within the concept of systems thinking the whole is greater than the sum of its parts (emergent properties).

A simple example of this is a bicycle. This is made up of a number of different systems: the gear system, the braking system, the transmission system, and so on. Each of these systems has an emergent property associated with its purpose. Depressing the brake lever will cause the brake blocks to close on the wheel rim and stop the wheel turning. None of these systems has the emergent property of the bicycle (the whole system), which is a machine that enables a human being to travel from A to B.

The following discussion helps to place this introduction in the context of the debates that have arisen in the management science and systems arenas from World War Two until the present day.

GENERAL SYSTEMS AND HARD SYSTEMS THINKING

Bertalanffy (1968) is considered as the founding father of General Systems Theory, having started to write and publish in the 1940s and 1950s. The early systems works developed largely from biological roots, and though they attempted to discover cross-discipline concepts that would relate to systems of all types, writing of the time tended to be couched in terms of biological analogies. Many different writers have explored more directly management related systems concepts in many different ways.

General systems thinking is interdisciplinary and is intended to provide an approach to enable understanding and analysis of complex systems, whether in nature, society, science or technology. In the context of this discussion, the term "system" refers to emergent purposeful activity, the boundaries of that activity, associated entities, and all of the relationships that exist between them in undertaking the sub-system activities needed for that system to exist. The system as a whole cannot be understood simply by studying its constituent parts. Systems thinking may be thought of as being about the organization of parts and their dynamic relationships, that comprise a whole, rather than the study of static organizational parts. This is counter to the traditional approach of Taylorism, which is based on classical assumptions (Taylor, 1911).

Within systems thinking phenomena may be considered as relationship networks within a boundary. The boundary encompasses the system, but the system has external connections, to other systems, and thus is considered open rather than closed. Common patterns, properties, and behaviors are key aspects of systems thinking. It is about looking at the whole rather than trying to solve each individual problem in isolation. Other key characteristics include emergence and hierarchy. Emergence has been mentioned previously and is the notion that a system will display at least one emergent property that none of its constituent parts can display individually. Hierarchy is the concept of systems within systems.

The Earth is a system within the Solar System, within the Milky Way, within the Universe. Within the Earth, the human being is a system. Within a human being are the respiratory, circulatory and other systems. Within these systems are the systems of molecules, and within these systems of atoms. Hierarchy in a systems sense does not imply the ranking that is found in the political sense. It is simply an order of connectivity between systems.

Bertalanffy (1968) was attempting to find a theory of general systems that would be able to address all systems in all scientific disciplines. He wished to use his observations from biology to describe attributes of systems in general. In particular, he argued that there are concepts and principles that may be applied generally to systems, regardless of their nature. He considered that there should be universal laws for general systems and not just theories that refer to specific types of systems. Bertalanffy (1968) identifies three major areas of systems thinking: philosophy, science and technology. Banathy (1966) considered four areas of enquiry that could be integrated. These are philosophy, theory, methodology and application, all integrating in a recursive relationship to make systems enquiry become knowledgeable action. Knowledgeable action is within the realm of KM.

From the concept of general systems came hard systems approaches. These assume that:

- well-defined problems exist that can be solved with a single optimal solution;
- a rigid scientific approach is the way to solve problems;

- everyone shares the same view of problems; and
- problems are technical in their nature.

Checkland (1981) suggests that systems thinking has the two complementary processes of systems analysis and systems synthesis. He argues that there are two paradigms related to these processes. The first views the world as systemic and it requires systematic study. The second views the world as problematic and it requires systemic study. In this case, problematic means "open to many different interpretations" (pluralistic). The first paradigm reflects hard systems thinking and the second reflects soft systems thinking.

Hard systems thinking works on the view that a problem can be solved by structuring a system to achieve the desired outcome. Typically such problems are quantifiable or technical. Systems analysis and systems engineering are forms of hard systems thinking. Structured Systems Analysis and Design Method (SSADM) is a particular hard systems approach that has been used for the design of information systems. This is a form of the more general Waterfall Model that views any development as flowing downwards through stages: requirements analysis, design, implementation, testing, integration and maintenance.

Hard systems thinking requires rational analysis, and as a scientific mode of investigation has limitations when transferred to social environments such as organizations. Key aspects of the hard systems approach are:

- reductionism, which is the process of simplifying the complex to define a specific experiment and provide a minimum explanation and analysis of a problem, component by component;
- experimentation in a controlled environment; and
- repeatability.

A major problem with the hard systems approach is its inability to cope with the complexity of social or organizational problems. For example, a reductionist approach requires simplification of problems by separating them into manageable parts resulting in experimentation and analysis being conducted in isolation from variables and external forces that could result in a different outcome. Such an approach does not consider changeable circumstances, and further, speculation cannot be accepted until experimentation and repeatability is achieved. As such, quantitative measures can be recorded and repeated more easily than qualitative findings. Hard systems thinking is goal directed and requires clearly defined problems to achieve solutions, with a philosophy based on ontology.

Considering hard systems in relation to KM, it is apparent that the ideas of a controlled environment and isolationist approach are inappropriate in what is essentially a social process. The concept of reductionism could be beneficial in the initial exploration of a complex area that involves people, processes, technology and environment. It is of little use if such areas are explored in total isolation from each other as each impacts significantly upon the other. Equally, experimentation and repeatability are not achievable in organizational contexts, as there will be different outcomes according to various internal and external influences. Other things cannot be "held equal" (remain the same) in an organization while one thing is changed to find out its effect.

SOFT SYSTEMS THINKING

Soft systems thinking aims at understanding problem situations and agreeing what problems exist, with a view to resolving the problem situation. Resolution, as opposed to solution, is the nature of soft systems thinking, and its philosophy is based on epistemology. Soft systems thinking is a holistic approach that recognizes organizations as complex social systems, and this view counters the conventional reductionist models that focus on departments and individuals as being separate from the whole. It is interdependence between individuals and groups, and the processes in which they engage, that help create a system.

Jackson (1993) provides an excellent background to the issues that led to the development of soft systems thinking:

> It was in the second world war that approaches such as operational research came into their own. These were used to help the allied war effort and quite successful they were . . . They assumed that people would share values . . . there are difficulties when you seek to extend the range of application of these approaches . . . Often the situation will be pluralistic, there will be different value positions, or it will be conflictual.

The successes of operational research during World War Two were expected to be mirrored in both private and public sector post-war organizations:

> In its heyday of the 1960s and early 1970s this approach was widely seen as the rational way to take decisions.
>
> (Rosenhead, 1989)

> It is, then, proposed that the development of man-machine digital systems be conducted as an applied scientific enterprise, regulated in accordance with an evolving set of hypotheses that relate systems design to systems performance, and are experimentally tested in anticipation of, and in response to, changing conditions.
>
> (Sackman, 1967)

The hopes for operational research were dented as a result of the more flexible and open social structures that existed in Western countries after World War Two. While technical problems suited a technique-oriented approach, many post-war organizational difficulties had much more to do with social science than physics:

> Unfortunately "management science" has not been able to resolve these problems. Hence there is an incentive to examine alternative paradigms to those of natural science, while continuing to build on the scientific bedrock: rationality applied to the findings of experience.
>
> (Checkland, 1981)

> . . . the basic philosophy and methodology of the "hard" systems approaches makes them unsuitable to applications in social situations, for there exists much corroborating evidence of failure in such situations.
>
> (Lewis, 1994: 27)

59

A much-quoted example of such hard systems failure is the RAND Corporation's experiences with the New York public health sector, using methods which had proved successful with the New York fire service (Greenberger *et al.*, 1976). A more recent example involved the failure of the London Ambulance Service Computer Aided Despatch system. The important thing to note from the findings is that it was not essentially a technical failure, but a failure with many causes, with a series of mistaken judgments. In particular, the report notes that senior managers lacked understanding as to how to manage this type of project, and there was failure to approach the development of the system in a totally open way (Prince User Group, Binder Hamlyn, 1993). In other words, a hard systems approach was mistakenly used to address a complex system involving human interaction.

Critics of OR in practice argue that failures have arisen because of OR's concentration on problems which have clearly defined, agreed objectives (e.g. Churchman, 1967; Ackoff, 1979). Partly, this perceived failure may arise through the difficulties associated with attempting to introduce change that is not in line with the organizational culture (Johnson *et al.*, 2007). Partly it may be linked to a lack of recognition of human factors, particularly in an IT environment (Boddy and Buchanan, 1992).

As a response to the issues that arose, a range of so-called "soft" methods have been developed over the last thirty years or so. Soft Systems Methodology (SSM) is regarded by some as a problem structuring exemplar (e.g. Rosenhead, 1989), and it is also one of the most widely-used and widely-known of the problem structuring methodologies (Mingers and Taylor, 1992). SSM was developed by Checkland (1981) and Wilson (1984), and was not based on any particular theory at that time. Checkland (1981) describes the complexity of social situations as compared to a scientific basis through three main features:

- Generalizations that might be made will be inaccurate in comparison to physical, quantitatively based controlled experiments.
- The researcher or investigator will always be an active participant in the situation being investigated resulting in personal perspectives, meanings and values. For example scientists' observations may include interpretations *for* others, the social scientist requires a sympathetic appreciation of the situation from the viewpoint of others.
- Making predictions about social situations is problematic, because although there might be particular outcomes intended, when these are observed and shared, through learning and increased knowledge with others the outcomes may change. In contrast, physical systems cannot react to predictions made about them.

From these observations and through action research, SSM developed as a learning process and is underpinned by four key principles, identified by Lehaney *et al.* (1999):

- holistic systems thinking based on the concepts of emergence and hierarchy, and communication and control;
- a learning rather than an optimizing approach to problem situations;
- relationship handling as opposed to goal achieving; and
- an action research paradigm.

Emergence, hierarchy, communication and control are core to systems thinking. Emergence relates to properties at a particular level, which cannot be reduced to lower levels for explanation, unlike the reductionist approach. Emergence *and* hierarchy together relate to emergent properties at particular layers in the structure of a system, which interact to make up the whole system. Communication and control relate to the overall direction and development of the system. All of this relates to the complete organization of a system, which is complex yet organized.

Checkland (1993: 280–281) uses Burrell and Morgan's (1979) framework (Figure 4.1) to draw out the social theory implicit in SSM, stating that it would lie in the left-hand quadrants with hermeneutics and phenomenology toward regulation. The left-hand quadrants relate to the subjective where social reality is perceived as having an existence that is a product of individual or shared consciousness. The subjective domain endeavors to seek knowledge by attempting to understand the views of others in creating social reality. At the extreme, people possess free will and the preferred method of gathering knowledge is by getting as close as possible to the subject under investigation.

Regulation is about understanding the status quo, with the perspective that society is basically consensual and change is generally incremental. Hermeneutics and phenomenology provide the philosophical base for interpretative studies. Interpretive sociology assumes that access to reality is only through social constructions such as language, consciousness and shared meanings. Interpretative studies generally attempt to understand phenomena through the meanings that people assign to them. Jackson (2000) points out that the combination of

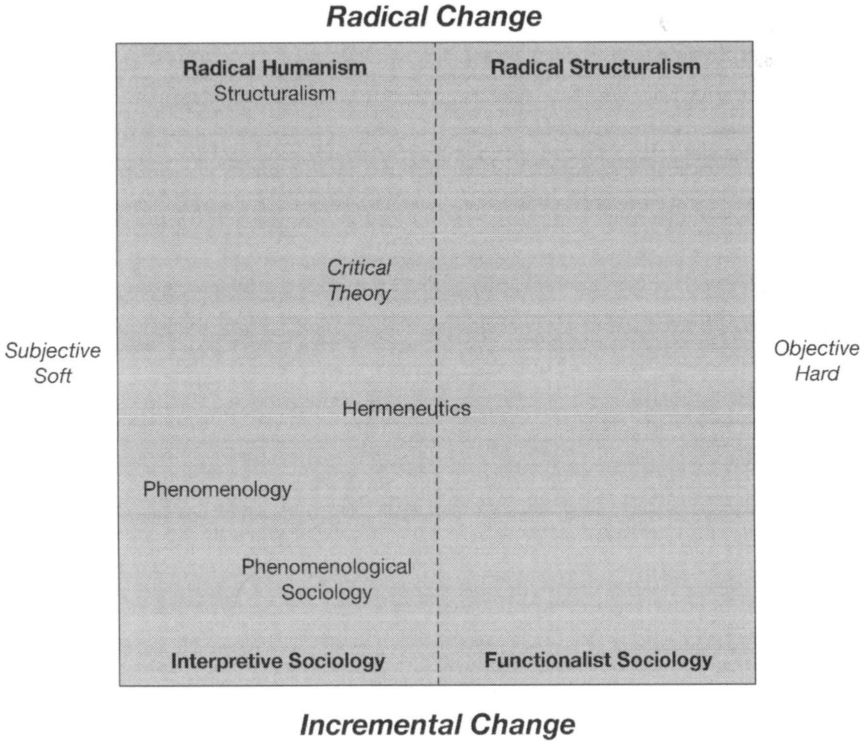

Radical Change

Radical Humanism Structuralism	**Radical Structuralism**
Critical Theory	
Hermeneutics	
Phenomenology	
Phenomenological Sociology	
Interpretive Sociology	**Functionalist Sociology**

Subjective Soft — *Objective Hard*

Incremental Change

Figure 4.1 *A Grid of Social Theory.*

Source: Burrell and Morgan (1979) in Checkland (1993: 280)

people and free will means that it is not normally possible to construct a model of such a system and the purpose is to understand the status quo better so that predictions and control can be better facilitated.

Hermeneutics is defined as knowledge gained by interpretation and became the established definition through Wilhelm Dilthey (1822–1911), who described it as historical, cultural and social facts that require interpretation and understanding. Considering this with KM, the knowledge cycle of gathering and interpreting information is influenced by the cultural and social present and past of an organization. It is contextualized by individuals or groups and enhances understanding and knowledge. Phenomenology has its origins in the work of Edmund Husserl (1859–1938) and is the attempt to describe experiences directly and independently of causal explanations. In this case, the relationship with the concept of KM may fall in the area of creativity and the notion of "thinking outside the box."

There have been many versions of SSM. Within the original version (Checkland, 1981) the unstructured problem situation is expressed, often by what is known as a "rich picture." This is used to search for relevant notional systems that are encapsulated as root definitions and conceptual models (4). Each conceptual model is compared with the "real world" in stage 5. The stage 5 comparison may undergo many iterations. Stage 4 originally included sub-sections 4a and 4b, which were formal and informal systems thinking inputs, but Checkland and Scholes (1990: 41–42) argue that with the development of CATWOE, 4a and 4b are not needed. (CATWOE—customer, actor, transformation, weltanschauung, owner, environment). Stage 6 is the assessment of changes that are both desirable and culturally feasible. Stage 7 is where action is taken to improve the situation (implementation). The cycle continues.

As an example of a root definition, consider the following definition of KM. Within this, the customer is not stated. The actors are the private or public concerns. The transformation (purpose) is to influence and achieve strategic aims. The weltanschauung (world view) is that using KM will do this better than not using KM. The owner is the public or private sector concern. The environmental constraints are financial, legal, resource, political, technical, cultural and societal:

> Knowledge management refers to the systematic organization, planning, scheduling, monitoring, and deployment of people, processes, technology, and environment, with appropriate targets and feedback mechanisms, under the control of a public or private sector concern, and undertaken by such a concern, to facilitate explicitly and specifically the creation, retention, sharing, identification, acquisition, utilization, and measurement of information and new ideas, in order more effectively to influence and achieve strategic aims, such as improved competitiveness or improved performance, subject to financial, legal, resource, political, technical, cultural, and societal constraints.
>
> (Lehaney et al., 2004)

The foregoing discussion considers SSM as a logical process. This logical process has a parallel cultural analysis: intervention or role analysis, social system analysis and political system analysis (Checkland and Scholes, 1990). Intervention (role) analysis considers the roles of client, would-be problem solver and problem owner. Social system analysis examines the problem situation as a culture, and the significance of social roles, norms and values within that culture. Political system analysis considers how power is obtained and disposed, and how that power is utilized in relationships between different interest groups.

Checkland (1993: 281) notes that SSM "covers the area in which Burrell and Morgan locate the critical theory of the Frankfurt School," for example the theory of Knowledge Constituitive Interests (Habermas, 1972). Habermas (1972) distinguishes between three primary cognitive experiences through which people create knowledge, termed technical, practical and emancipatory interests. These areas define cognitive experiences or learning domains and are grounded in different aspects of social existence—work, interaction and power.

The technical interest is linked to work, and involves people achieving goals and material wellbeing. The technical interest is especially concerned with prediction, control and manipulation of the physical world. The generation of knowledge in this case is based on instrumental action using empirical analytical methods within the positivistic sciences, e.g. physics, chemistry and biology.

The practical domain identifies human social interaction or communicative action, involving mutual expectations, understanding of participants and debate. The criterion of clarification of conditions for communication and understanding of meaning is used to determine what action is appropriate. The practical domain falls within the historical hermeneutic methods; for example, social sciences, history, legal, etc.

The emancipatory interest relates to coercion and power, which can hinder (or help) the progression of work and interaction. This domain identifies self-reflection and involves one's own history, social conditioning, values and norms. The emancipation refers to the ability to free oneself from environmental constraints, power of others over self and the awareness necessary to release oneself from such constraints. The importance of the emancipatory interest can be seen in debate, which occurs in the practical interest. A debate that does not deal with the concept of emancipation will develop under constraint and stunt a beings potential for development. Knowledge in the emancipatory domain is generated through self-reflection leading to a change in consciousness and perspective.

Applying Habermas' Knowledge Constituitive Interests to SSM, SSM falls primarily within the practical domain because it is aimed at consensual debate, which explores alternative Weltanschauungen and has criteria of success established through action research.

Comparing SSM, KM and Habermas' Knowledge Constituitive interests, the components may be linked as per Table 4.1.

Table 4.1 *Knowledge Constituitive Interests, SSM and Knowledge Management*

Knowledge Constituitive Interests	SSM	Knowledge Management
Technical—prediction, control, manipulation of physical world	Primary task root definitions.	Technical control of objectified processes—use of IT and clearly defined system to share information. (KM Process)
Practical debate, participation	Issue based root definitions. Learning cycle, CATWOE	Maintaining, creating, communicating, and improving knowledge. (KM Activities)
Emancipatory—power and politics	Political analysis	Critical reflection, understanding and freedom to create and share knowledge. (KM Development)

SSM and soft systems thinking in general are, however, open to critique. This critique led to a development known as critical systems thinking. This will be discussed on p. 66.

CASE EXERCISE: INTERVENTION IN AN OUTPATIENT'S DEPARTMENT

This case is drawn from Lehaney *et al.* (1999)

In the U.K., publicly funded hospitals (National Health Service or NHS) run outpatient clinics. These enable patients who have been referred by their general practitioner (family doctor) or from elsewhere in the hospital, to receive diagnosis, treatment and prognosis within a scheduled appointment. The nominal appointment duration is ten minutes, but in practice the appointment might take from five to thirty minutes.

The work attempted to address gaps between customers' and providers' expectations and the intervention used a soft systems approach, coupled with simulation modeling. Simulation modeling is a means by which the activities and entities in a system, and their relationships, can be captured, usually on a computer, and usually with graphics that represent what is going on in the system.

The hospital faced some issues that it had to address. In particular, patients were queuing (waiting in line) for longer than was desired. There were also concerns about the number of patients who did not turn up for appointments (did-not-attends, or DNAs).

The intervention was initiated as a result of UK Government pressure on the NHS to improve its service. This was as a result of a number of factors, including increasing pressures on health service expenditure driven by advances in medical treatment, social pressures such as the elderly living longer, and the inefficiencies of such a large public sector organization. An NHS Performance Guide is published annually (from 1993–1994), and this indicates how local health services are performing. For each hospital, outpatient statistics show the percentage of patients seen within thirty minutes of appointment time, and this is a key statistic.

Long outpatient queues in the NHS were not new, but the pressure to reduce them was. The task was to reduce such queues, but without using additional resources. It is not a straightforward challenge, as having queues of patients avoids the possibility of doctors having to wait for the next patient to arrive. Given that doctors are an extremely expensive resource, this is an unacceptable scenario.

Through existing networks, we met with the Associate Director of Information Services (Associate Director) of a local NHS Trust. He felt that "pressure to perform" had increased in recent years, and was searching for ways to make noticeable improvements. He was not clear as to what, where and how. We felt that such case material would be useful for us in many ways, and we agreed that mutual benefit might be gained by collaboration on a research project. At this stage, the Associate Director appeared to be in the roles of client, would-be problem solver and problem owner, while we were would-be problem solvers and would-be problem owners.

The Consultant Dermatologist was a major participant and if improvements to performance could be made at this outpatients' clinic, it might be possible that similar issues could be addressed elsewhere. A second meeting with the Associate Director, the Consultant Dermatologist (Consultant), the Outpatients Department Manager (Manager) and the Senior Ward Sister (Sister) was held, and it became very clear that if any one of these individuals withdrew co-operation the intervention could not continue. Hence they are termed "key stakeholders."

The intervention was undertaken in four linked stages. Cultural analysis was done in Stage 1. In this, the roles of the participants and the social and political systems were considered. This enabled soft objectives to be set and the nature of the project and likely timescales to be agreed. The areas were considered against desirability, feasibility and participants' expectations and observations.

In Stage 2 the group favored the use of simple flowcharts, which were compared with participants' expectations and observations and adjusted as work progressed. These flowcharts were extremely useful in many ways, not least because they helped the participants gain a greater understanding of their own organization. Eventually, most of the charts were dropped in favor of a flowchart of the patients' experiences from entering the clinic to leaving. The reasoning was that this was the one area that the group could influence with any hope of success.

The key stakeholders were keen to see a computer simulation model, and a series of iterations took place involving the flowcharts and computer models. Eventually flowcharts were dropped and development took place solely on computer models. Flowcharts provided only a static representation of the systems, whereas computer simulation models would enable dynamic depictions.

In Stage 3, simulation modeling began and models were compared with expectations and observations, and adjusted accordingly. The desirable and feasible outcomes of Stage 3 were that operational (process) actions were taken to reduce both queuing times and the incidence of patients not attending. Patient waiting time and doctor utilization were reaffirmed as the major issues for consideration, and simulation models were built to mimic patient arrival to patient departure. A prototyping approach was used in building the models until a satisfactory outcome was achieved.

Stage 4 moved the project on from operational to strategic level. Instead of the simulation helping solve a single problem, a system of intervention was developed and agreed to help address ongoing complex situations. The intervention resulted in a procedure to reduce unexpected non-attendance of patients, and a system to schedule patient bookings according to simple rules was developed, with an associated reduction in clinic waiting times. In order to achieve these things it was important to address the overall situation as more than a technical problem. The technical issues were important but equally important were the perceptions of those involved in running the clinic. Based on this, key stakeholders helped develop and accepted the simulation models, and a model of the intervention process itself, which they hoped to use for continuing investigations. In addition, participants increased their knowledge of their own systems.

CRITICAL SYSTEMS THINKING

SSM has been criticized for not fully addressing the issue of political domination and emancipation. For example, Mingers (1984) argues that two forms of subjectivism, strong and weak, should be considered. He suggests that pure, strong subjectivism that does not allow for the possibility of some extra individual reality, creates a weakness in the value of SSM, as any one view of the world is as valid as any other. In addition, the proposition that the world is socially constructed must also be a socially constructed view. Mingers goes on to advocate weak subjectivism in which the subject is emphasized, but extra individual structures are accepted. This subjectivist stance raises criticisms of the ability of SSM to be utilized as a tool of radical change, as social norms might work to preserve the status quo.

Recognition of this is important because if an organization wishes to engage in KM, it requires understanding about its own human activity systems. In particular, the recognition of social constraints and obstructions is important if progress is to be made to free individuals and groups from political issues that may impede the successful implementation of KM. Such issues may be considered through the theory of Knowledge Constituitive Interests (Habermas, 1972), which has provided much of the basis for critical systems thinking.

Critical theory assumes that social reality is historically constructed. Critical theory suggests that although people are constrained by various forms of social, cultural and political constraints, exposing such constraints is necessary to achieve emancipation. If KM involves innovation and creativity to think and produce beyond individual experiences, then social, cultural and political domination should be key considerations. Ulrich (1983) describes Habermas' theory of Knowledge Constituitive Interests as the process of learning, gaining experience and knowledge through different contexts and action, influenced by social and historical experience.

Critical systems thinking attempts to bring together systems thinking and participatory methods to help address boundary judgments and complexity. Just as SSM is one approach within soft systems thinking, Critical Systems Heuristics (CSH) is an approach within critical systems thinking. CSH was developed by Ulrich (1983), and it focuses on discovering whose interest a system serves by examining any assumptions and values associated with the system, and the purpose of the system. To be critical is to be "self reflective in respect to the presuppositions flowing into one's own judgments, both in the search for true knowledge and rational action" (Ulrich, 1983: 20). CSH uses questions relating to control, expertise, legitimization and motivation. The idea is that these may help expose and free the design from individual organizational, cultural, societal and political value assumptions that may be hidden and coercive. In this way CSH lays claims to being an emancipatory approach. In terms of KM, the design should include consideration for individual, organizational, cultural, societal and political issues, and how these might be addressed and dealt with in an organization.

Critical Systems Heuristics studies existing or planned systems, from a point of view of discovering whose interests the system serves. It considers the assumptions and values associated with the system (or proposed system). It uses "boundary questions," such as "What is the actual purpose of the system design?" These questions are aimed at the system planners and also the people affected by the system. The power of the questions to reveal the normative content of the system design is best seen if they are put in "is" mode and "ought" mode. Thus, the questions, "Who *is* the actual client of the systems design?" and "Who *ought* to be the client of the systems design?" would be asked. The boundary questions are designed to highlight sources of control, expertise, legitimacy and motivation (Jackson, 1992: 191). These can then be used by planners, and others involved in the situation, to show underlying value assumptions of the system design. The purpose is to expose, and hopefully free, the design from individual, organizational, cultural, societal and political value assumptions that may be hidden and coercive. By doing this, it is using an emancipatory systems approach. This revealing of "true" motives in a planning situation may itself lead to new planning proposals.

Ulrich (1987) proposes a list of twelve questions. Each question is to be asked in the "is" mode and the "ought" mode, thus making twenty-four questions in total. The questions are within the domains of four basic boundary issues, which are as follows:

- The basis of motivation: where does a sense of purposefulness and value come from?
- The basis of power: who is in control of what is going on and is needed for success?
- The basis of knowledge: what experience and expertise support the claim?
- The basis of legitimacy: where does legitimacy lie?

Questions 1–9 are about those involved with issues. Questions 10–12 are about those affected by issues. Tables 4.2–4.5 (from Ulrich, 1987) provide a checklist of boundary questions.

While CSH purports to be emancipatory, it can be argued that this methodology does not contribute enough to how any changes, by which the design is freed of hidden value assumptions, are undertaken. Some doubt the efficacy of the methodology, on the grounds that it neglects the structural aspects and development of social systems favored in a strucuralist analysis.

Table 4.2 *Sources of Motivation*

(1) Who is (ought to be) the client or beneficiary? That is, whose interests are (should be) served?

(2) What is (ought to be) the purpose? That is, what are (should be) the consequences?

(3) What is (ought to be) the measure of improvement or measure of success? That is, how can (should) we determine that the consequences, taken together, constitute an improvement?

(Source: Ulrich, 1987)

Table 4.3 *Sources of Power*

(4) Who is (ought to be) the decision-maker? That is, who is (should be) in a position to change the measure of improvement?

(5) What resources and other conditions of success are (ought to be) controlled by the decision-maker? That is, what conditions of success can (should) those involved control?

(6) What conditions of success are (ought to be) part of the decision environment? That is, what conditions can (should) the decision-maker not control (e.g. from the viewpoint of those not involved)?

(Source: Ulrich, 1987)

Table 4.4 *Sources of Knowledge*

(7) Who is (ought to be) considered a professional or further expert? That is, who is (should be) involved as competent providers of experience and expertise?

(8) What kind expertise is (ought to be) consulted? That is, what counts (should count) as relevant knowledge?

(9) What or who is (ought to be) assumed to be the guarantor of success? That is, where do (should) those involved seek some guarantee that improvement will be achieved—for example, consensus among experts, the involvement of stakeholders, the experience and intuition of those involved, political support?

(Source: Ulrich, 1987)

Table 4.5 *Sources of Legitimation*

(10) Who is (ought to be) witness to the interests of those affected but not involved? That is, who is (should be) treated as a legitimate stakeholder, and who argues (should argue) the case of those stakeholders who cannot speak for themselves, including future generations and non-human nature?

(11) What secures (ought to secure) the emancipation of those affected from the premises and promises of those involved? That is, where does (should) legitimacy lie?

(12) What worldview is (ought to be) determining? That is, what different visions of "improvement" are (should be) considered, and how are they (should they be) reconciled?

(Source: Ulrich, 1987)

CONCLUSIONS AND SUMMARY

This chapter discussed general systems thinking, hard systems thinking, soft systems thinking and critical systems thinking. It has provided an overview of these and developed some links with KM. System thinking has a range of methodologies or approaches for addressing interventions, and two of these, Soft Systems Methodology and Critical Systems Heuristics, have been outlined. The links between Knowledge Constituitive Interests, Soft Systems Methodology and KM have been tabulated.

Hard systems thinking may be appropriate for technical or quantitative problems that can have an optimal solutions. Soft systems thinking is to do with problem situations and the resolution (rather than solution) of those. Critical systems thinking attempts to address emancipation, and the defining of roles and interests within contexts. Each of these forms of systems thinking may have something to offer to KM. Each may be criticized in various ways.

The work in this area is not fully developed as it is a fairly recent innovation, but it would appear that systems thinking and KM may be complementary, and may be stronger together than separately.

REVIEW QUESTIONS

1 In general, what is systems thinking about?

2 Why did soft systems thinking develop?

3 What is the main approach within soft systems thinking covered in this chapter?

4 What is the main approach within critical systems thinking covered within this chapter?

5 What are the two modes of enquiry in Critical Systems Heuristics?

DISCUSSION QUESTIONS

1 How can systems thinking be linked to KM?

2 Why might this potentially be useful?

3 How might systems thinking and KM be used together in a past, present or future work situation?

CASE EXERCISE: COMPANY X'S IS DEPARTMENT (XIS)[4]

This case exercise outlines a perspective of KM and then uses that perspective to critically appraise experiences of the activities of Company X's IS department. It looks at how and where knowledge is communicated and the possible opportunities and barriers to improving KM within the department.

Background

It is widely agreed that we are entering a knowledge economy and society, and the ability to manage knowledge has been proved to be the most critical thing for an organization to survive and maintain its competitive advantage (Shariq, 1997). It has also been recognized that there is a trend in economies towards greater value accruing from intangible resources (Machlup, 1980).

Sharp (2003) states that as a consequence of this economic trend, the fields of intellectual capital and KM have burgeoned in significance among academics and practitioners. It is reasonable to argue that widespread interest in KM both as an academic subject and as business issue dates from the mid-1990s. Early authors such as Stewart, Wiig and Sveiby published their first works around 1990 (Grant, 2007).

Despite recent focus, KM in a practical form has been with us for us as far back as we can go; humans by their nature learn from their experiences, and pass those experiences among their peers, and down across generations—this is arguably what separates us from other species and has allowed civilization to develop. Wiig (1997) muses that the first hunters surely were concerned about the expertise and skills of their team mates when they went out to capture prey. They also, he surmises, ascertained that what they knew as the best and most successful practices were taught to up-and-coming hunters to ensure the viability of the group.

From very early times, wise people have secured sustained succession by transferring in-depth knowledge to the next generation. If we take a moment to reflect on how we as a species have matured, we might think to look at some of the more philosophical writings on evolution. Kropotkin (1902) states:

> In the practice of mutual aid, which we can retrace to the earliest beginnings of evolution, we thus find the positive and undoubted origin of our ethical conceptions; and we can affirm that in the ethical progress of man, mutual support not mutual struggle — has had the leading part. In its wide extension, even at the present time, we also see the best guarantee of a still loftier evolution of our race.

It could be argued that the evolution derived from mutual support could only be achieved if that mutual support had a foundation that shared and learnt from experience. Charles Darwin's views around the "survival of the fittest" add further support to this line of argument. We may have to concede that, whether conscious or otherwise, KM has existed for longer than recent interest might suggest.

What is Knowledge?

Before we can understand KM, we first have to draw some consensus on how we might define Knowledge. We can use the DIKW model put forward by Ackoff (1989) to understand how we arrive at Knowledge; it describes the chain of actions that lead to and supersede Knowledge (see Figure 1.2 on p. 6). As a summary of current understanding:

- Data comes in the form of raw observations and measurements.
- Information is created by analyzing relationships and connections between the data. It answers the "who, what, where" style questions.
- Knowledge is created by using the information for action. Knowledge answers the question "how." Knowledge is a local practice or relationship that works.
- Wisdom is created through use of knowledge, through the communication of knowledge users, and through reflection. Wisdom answers the questions "why" and "when" as they relate to actions. Wisdom deals with the future, as it takes context and consequence into account.

The *Oxford English Dictionary* (*OED*) describes Knowledge as:

1 Information and skills acquired through experience or education.
2 The sum of what is known.
3 Awareness or familiarity gained by experience of a fact or situation: he denied all knowledge of the incident.

Blackler (1995) considers Knowledge to be a wider dimension than this description purveys — he describes knowledge as "multifaceted and complex, being both situated and abstract, implicit and explicit, distributed and individual, physical and mental, developing and static, verbal and encoded."

It is this type of description that forms the basis of much of the research around KM—just how do you capture and manage an entity that exists across a matrix of tangible and intangible properties?

The tangible and intangible aspects of Knowledge are represented by two defined states, tacit and explicit. Polanyi (1966) defines tacit knowledge as implied, but is not actually documented, nevertheless the individual "knows" it from experience, from other people, or from a combination of sources. Polanyi (1967) later states that tacit knowledge focuses on personal knowledge rooted in individual experience and involving personal belief, perspective and values; whereas explicit knowledge describes aspects that are recorded or formal.

Skyrme and Amidon (1997) define explicit knowledge as formal, systematic and objective, an entity that is generally codified in words or numbers. Explicit knowledge can be acquired from a number of sources, including company-internal data, business processes, records of policies and procedures, as well as from external sources such as intelligence gathering. Tacit knowledge is more intangible. It resides in an individual's brain and forms the basis on which individuals make decisions and take actions, but it is not externalized in any form.

Kane *et al.* (2006) identify the distinction between these two aspects by listing the characteristics of each:

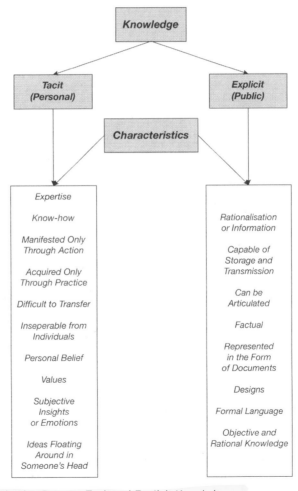

Figure E *The Distinction Between Tacit and Explicit Knowledge.*

Based on these characteristics, wisdom (as depicted in the DIKW model), could be viewed as the crossover between explicit and tacit knowledge or the point at which knowledge becomes personal, is context specific and therefore hard to formalize and communicate (Bali, 2008a).

An Understanding of Knowledge Management

KM refers to the allocation of knowledge assets as a means to improve organizational processes. KM approaches include the resources, methods and instruments to deliver KM goals. KM goals are usually described in terms of knowledge assets. Due to the nature of knowledge assets, organizational processes tend to improve as knowledge assets are shared and leveraged among organizational members (Weber, 2007). Fundamentally, knowledge-based activities include the creation and integration of knowledge, and accumulation and utilization of knowledge, and the learning and sharing of knowledge and together these comprise KM (Shieh-Chieh *et al.*, 2005).

Bali (2008b) states that KM is intended to facilitate explicitly and specifically the:

- creation;
- retention;
- sharing;
- identification;
- acquisition;
- utilization; and
- measurement of information and new ideas

in order to achieve strategic aims, such as improved competitiveness.

If we accept that knowledge is more than a tangible entity, that it also exists as an intangible and personal instinct, drawn from a person's experiences and contextualized reaction in reference to a particular paradigm (Marakas, 1999), then the concept of KM covers a wide spectrum. It is more than the logical and systematic capture of information into codified knowledge. It is the consequence of the interaction between people, their experiences, their instincts (arguably based on their experiences) and the surroundings in which they operate. By providing an environment that facilitates and stimulates this interaction, it could be viewed that we are practicing in KM.

Bhatt (2001) states that to capitalize on knowledge, an organization must be swift in balancing its KM activities. In general, such a balancing act requires changes in organizational culture, techniques and technologies. A number of organizations believe that by focusing exclusively on a single entity from within the group people, techniques and technology, they can manage knowledge. However, by exclusively focusing on only one of these entities the organization does not put its self in a position of being able to sustain competitive advantage. It is, rather, the interaction between these entities that allow an organization to manage knowledge effectively. By creating a nurturing and "learning-by-doing" type of environment, an organization can sustain its competitive advantage.

Echoing the points made by Bhatt diagrammatically, Bali (2008a) presents a graphic (see Figure 1.1 on p. 2)—it must be recognized that each area has an overlap and thus a requirement for interdependence. If we look into each of these elements, their interfaces and interdependencies, we can begin to gain a more rounded interpretation of KM as an activity.

Looking at a higher level, Emery (1959) and Trist (1981) provide the view that the conversion between data and information is efficiently handled through Information Technologies, but IT is a poor substitute for converting information into knowledge. The conversion between information and knowledge is best accomplished through people, but people are slow in converting data to information. This is one of the reasons they believe that KM is best carried out through the optimization of technology and social subsystems.

One the key requirements to expand and develop knowledge across an organization is the provision of a platform that can facilitate the collation and dissemination of data and information, to allow it to become a knowledge resource. Technology can provide a platform to physically enable activities, and has an array of options that can be utilized. E-mail, intranet, news-groups, instant messaging and bulletin boards all provide vehicles that can support the distribution of knowledge across an organization.

Using these mediums users can discuss, debate and interpret information through multiple perspectives. However, Glasser (1998) has identified that changing people's behavior is one of the critical implementation problems in KM, because KM projects force a company to redefine its traditional work procedures, power structures and technologies. This indicates that before benefits can be gained from the physical platforms provided by technology and the route ways defined by process, we have to first re-program the user community to understand the benefits.

This re-programming requires an approach that addresses the point that individuals learn at different speeds and levels. Bateson (1972) identified that there are several fundamental levels of learning, each being more abstract yet having a greater degree of influence on the overall objective. Dilts (1996) interpreted these abstractions to the following:

Table 4.6 *Levels of Learning*

Level	Note
2. *Spiritual*	"Self actualization"—seeking further knowledge to improve the activity
4. *Identity*	Becoming an advocate and a sponsor for the activity
6. *Beliefs*	Practicing the activity and reaping the benefits. "getting it"
8. *Capabilities*	Understanding how to practice the activity, the benefits and limitations
10. *Behaviors*	Understanding the rules, processes and expectations
12. *Environment*	Setting the scene, and understanding the enablers

If we review these levels against the three entities identified as being instrumental in the delivery of successful KM (people, processes and technologies), we can observe that, whereas at the lower levels there could be some influence from technology and process, the higher levels are much more people focused.

If we apply this line of thinking to the integration of KM we could conclude that technology, however efficient, has little use unless its operators believe in the benefits of using it; assuming that they simply won't, we could use process to create the behaviors that mandate usage (which to some extent would create capability from an organizational perspective), but if ultimately individuals have no belief, then any KM initiative has a probability of failure. To succeed, the active community has to be educated to KM's benefits and given the right environment in which to undertake its delivery.

If the user community is to entertain the notion of "re-programming," then they will require motivation to do so. Such motivation is a strong element that will lead to the adoption of a KM culture; just because an individual understands the benefits, it still doesn't guarantee that they will choose to practice the activity. KM is as much about giving as it is about receiving—for our knowledge, and ultimately the wider community's knowledge to grow, we have to be prepared to share our ideas, thoughts and experiences; otherwise we cannot learn from each other and accelerate the growth of knowledge.

People will have different levels of motivation that will encourage them to become a "knowledge worker." Nelson (1994) points to a study carried out by Kenneth Kovach where 1,000 employees and 100 of their bosses were asked to list the things that they believe motivated employees. The two lists did not overlap. Bosses believed that their employees were motivated by good salaries and job security, while their employees gave factors that included participating in interesting work, feeling appreciated at work and "being a part of things."

Job security and good wages were ranked as important but were lower down. Maslow (1954) puts forward a hierarchy of needs that concurs with Kovach's findings. At the bottom of Maslow's pyramid are the most basic human needs such as food and shelter; things which motivate us to get out of bed and go to work. Once these basic needs are met, Maslow claims that we are motivated by higher factors, such as autonomy and self-esteem. What this indicates is that motivation is personal, and each individual will have different reasons to be motivated.

In conclusion, KM is wider than the systematic storage of codified knowledge; it has aspects that are heavily people focused. For it to be a success, the user community involved needs to be enabled. Those enablers come from three key areas: facilitation, motivation and education. It requires the user community to be neutered and encouraged towards a belief system that is facilitated by technology and process. KM will work if people want it to work—that "want" can ultimately be achieved through education and motivation. The challenge is tailoring that education and motivation at the correct level for the individual.

The IS Department

This entity is supported by an IT application portfolio of circa 250 systems, a number of which are required to have 24/7 availability. The majority of applications are bespoke, being developed and maintained by an in-house team (XIS). XIS has around 140 employees and contractors, primarily consisting of managers, analysts, developers and DBAs, and operational support staff.

XIS has to remain in-tune with the requirements of the business, and factor those requirements against advances in technology that can create additional efficiencies. As an example, changes within the energy industry will have a big impact on the existing application portfolio. The current application portfolio will need to be revised and improved to meet new business requirements, a task that will rely heavily on the knowledge of XIS's human resources.

Knowledge within XIS

The role of knowledge within XIS is important to the department's performance. At a basic level those knowledge requirements break down as follows:

Table 4.7 *XIS's Knowledge Requirements*

Department	Task	Knowledge requirement
General	Activity flows and interfaces	In-house processes In-house systems People—who does what
Strategy	Devise the program of work	Business activities Industry best practice Current application health
Strategy	Devise development and architecture standards	Technology developments Corporate standards
Development	Devise specific projects	Business activities Project methodologies Application architecture
Development	Extract detailed user requirements	Business activities Analysis standards and techniques
Development	Technical design	Application architecture Development standards and techniques
Development	Build	Application architecture Development standards and techniques Coding standards and constructs
Development	Testing	Business activities Application architecture Testing techniques
Operations	Support	Business activities (priorities) Application architecture
Operations	Maintenance	Application architecture Development standards and techniques Coding standards and constructs

Obtaining and managing this knowledge requirement in the current environment is challenging. KM as a discipline is not formally recognized within XIS. There are aspects of day-to-day activities that could be considered as being within the boundaries of KM, but none exist as part of any larger initiative or framework.

Methodologies and frameworks are adopted for systems development and support activities; with a core set of processes being defined, and loosely followed, to apply some structure and governance to the application of those activities. The primary measure to indicate the success of any processes is that XIS satisfies the auditors that it is compliant within the rigors of the Sarbanes-Oxley (SOX) Act.

Although Company X has now de-listed from the U.S. Stock Exchange (which mandates SOX), the company made the decision to continue with the SOX audit—largely because it is the only external audit of activities, and internally staff are familiar with the approach. In reality, an annual pre-audit push is made to ensure that the audit is passed, which is how I justify my earlier comment that processes are "loosely followed." If there was belief and commitment to the purpose, there would be no requirement for the pre-audit push. At any level, SOX does little to support the growth of knowledge as it is concerned more with the existence of artifacts than the actual quality.

Earlier in this report, I expressed that KM was the consequence of the success and interdependence between three key areas: People, Technology and Process—the following looks at each of these areas from the perspective of XIS activities.

People

Within XIS, the core knowledge exists as an interaction between its user communities. The quickest and easiest way to understand "what, where, when, who and how" is to identify and hold a dialogue with the relevant knowledge holder. Any codified knowledge stored in the form of documentation, is typically seen as difficult to locate, unreliable, out of date or simply non-existent; for this reason, documentation simply isn't trusted, quite often, anything that is codified is bypassed in favor of face-to-face discussions with the right people.

Initially the right people are in position because of focused recruitment campaigns, targeting and ultimately employing individuals that bring the right knowledge to the vacant role. However much experience an individual brings to a role, that experience needs to be contextualized to fit with the environment within which their role exists. Their explicit knowledge learnt from education and previous assignments, needs localization to become tacit and ultimately of true benefit to XIS—something that within the current "people centric" culture takes a lot longer than arguably it should.

The lack of trust for the current documentation is down to people—as ultimately it is their responsibility to codify the explicit aspects of their knowledge. As much as a person may try to dissuade direct approaches to uncover their knowledge, if that same person chooses not to codify and, probably more importantly, actively campaign for stronger KM, then they are perpetuating the current culture.

In my experience, KM is an area that everybody within XIS appears to recognize the need for, and the benefits of achieving—but nobody is willing to take up the responsibility for delivering it. There is insufficient motivation to encourage knowledge sharing; the consequence is that individuals and small communities build up their own knowledge repositories.

In paradox, Company X operates a corporate-wide program ("Program"), which is focused on building and sustaining motivation. The Program works by defining the objectives and development requirements that will drive the organization forward. Based on these requirements, goals are cascaded down to define targets for each employee; those targets are then measured and the overall level attained determines the size of annual bonus that an individual can attain.

A regular dialogue takes place between individuals and their managers to assess progress against defined targets, with one of the key roles of the manager being to sustain motivation. As formal recognition of knowledge-based activities does not currently exist as any targeted set of goals, they fall outside of the formal "motivational" structure.

The Program also rewards individual development, supporting and encouraging employees to increase their knowledge through vocational and academic pursuit. In the technology-driven environment that IT is, it is important that individuals maintain an up-to-date perspective on technology and industry best practice. The explicit knowledge provided by education, once contextualized against the business, should develop the tacit knowledge that will deliver competitive advantage. By encouraging the growth of its employees, Company X looks to position itself as a "learning organization," which should in turn perpetuate its growth.

From a KM perspective, the Program provides a formal structure that maximizes the organization's potential to sustain growth by focusing employees and developing employees to achieve the task in hand. It also provides the framework to target an individual's motivation and education towards the success of any adopted initiatives and business directives.

Techniques

Company X recognizes the role of best practice, and on the surface it has good intention to adopt that best practice. It has adapted processes, methodologies, templates and frameworks to facilitate and guide its community to work in a uniform and pragmatic manner.

The reality is that few of these are followed with any discipline, people are not sufficiently educated or motivated to do that following, so they develop their own routes and shortcuts. Members of the XIS community need better education, not just as to what they have to do, but why they have to do it, and then suitable motivation to sustain what they have learnt. Otherwise people just don't recognize the benefits or the consequence of their actions, and arguably don't care enough to change the way they work. Their actions may allow them to undertake their own tasks with expedience, but when others rely on the knowledge outcome of those tasks they don't assist the wider community.

One key area where process is often bypassed is an area that should support the growth of knowledge—documentation; the laying down and imparting of explicit artifacts that others can use to build their own knowledge. The Committee on Human Factors for the National Research Council (1987) has observed that the problem with documentation is that it is often easier to undertake then document. Often the documentation never gets done because it simply isn't viewed as critical to the undertaking.

As a department there is an acceptance that, although not perfect, XIS performs. The tacit understanding of who, what, where, when and how overrides the elements that are explicit. It could be argued that the growth of knowledge and the collective learning of XIS is facilitated by the flexibility that is afforded to the community, although through that flexibility the organization leaves itself vulnerable to the individuals within that community; it is a risk that seemingly senior managers are happy to accept. Once an individual is integrated into the existing culture, they perpetuate the cycle by creating their own shortcuts—and are free to do so. This is not to say that processes, methodologies, etc. are completely by-passed because they are not, they are flexed or interpreted to the user's best interest—with little or no scrutinized measures in place to identify and dissuade to the contrary.

Technologies

Little exists to support KM within XIS, and those technologies that do exist, as was outlined in "Techniques," are operated with a degree of flexibility that doesn't maximize their knowledge capabilities.

The primary "formal" knowledge silo that exists for XIS is within *Documentum*. *Documentum* is a document management system that provides a hierarchical storage system, version control and security. If used as defined by "Techniques," it would hold all project and support documentation, be up to date and be the first port of call for explicit knowledge-related queries. There are a number of reasons why *Documentum* is not used as it is intended:

- Insufficient governance over processes—people don't use it and are not challenged.
- Lack of trust in the technology—it can be slow, and occasionally out of service.

- Permissions are not correctly applied—users can't access/view what they want.
- Poor structure—no governance over how it has been used, so it can be difficult to locate something (assuming it exists).
- Lacks of training—users don't have sufficient understanding of how to use it, or how it should be laid out.

XIS operates with the support of a conventional infrastructure, including networked PCs and telecommunications equipment—all of which facilitate the sharing of knowledge. They also add further opportunity to bypass the use of *Documentum*.

E-mail is the primary communication tool that forms the nucleus of probably all user groups. It is the first application opened in the morning, and the last one closed at night. Most of all knowledge that could and should be codified and centrally located will exist within somebody's e-mail. In addition to e-mail, users are able to create shared folders on as common (shared) drive. Users have full access to this drive to create folders, save documents and share documents—all within that user's own personal structure. So unless you know where something exists, or you are provided with the location—it would be difficult to find (assuming it was there to find in the first place).

In addition to document management, XIS operates an application called *Remedy* for incident management. Issues are raised by the business and entered into *Remedy* as tickets, those tickets are then resolved and closed—with some brief explanation as to how the issue was resolved being added to the ticket. The information written into a ticket cannot be easily recalled and is not searchable—so if there is a problem with application X, again there is no way to re-call previous problems to 1: find the solution and 2: identify common threads.

Support relies heavily on the knowledge of its personnel. The effectiveness of the team comes from "what you know," followed by "who you know." I joined Company X as a senior member of the XIS support team, and my previous knowledge was of little use until I had built up my "tacit" knowledge base—with little explicit codified knowledge to draw on, this took a lot longer than it should have and, at times, was frustrating.

This is a repeated story with each new user and something that the organization is yet to learn from—an irony for an organization that uses the Program to promote learning and development.

Consequences

In May 2007, Company X announced the decision to merge seven of its existing business units trading departments, currently spread across Europe, into a single, new business unit—Company X Trading (XET); the further decision was made to locate that business unit in Germany. XET is expected to complete the physical integration of the seven departments over a phased period, with the logical integration (single processes) expected to be completed by the end of 2010. For XIS, this has brought about a number of challenges; from a knowledge perspective, the primary challenge is that a large number of its current staff are not prepared to move to Germany, which is supplemented by the further decision that knowledgeable contractors will also not be a part of the migration. This has posed an important question:

> How does the organization support and maintain its existing application portfolio, when the current knowledgeable base for that portfolio is heavily people focused—and those people will no longer be available?

This issue, it transpires, is not isolated to XIS; it is present in some form within each of the migrating departments. The current solution has been to appoint a third party supplier to integrate into each of the current business units, to carry out a number of systems appreciation exercises with the view that they will be in a position to play a "bridging" support role (if required) while XET's IS function build up its own internal capability. The second outcome is the creation of a central knowledge base, which will be developed and maintained as an integrated service to the performing XET's IS function.

The harvesting, interpretation and presentation of the organizations existing knowledge has come at a not insignificant cost, and is still an activity that is in progress and has yet to prove that it will fully mitigate the initial risk. Had XIS, and its wider European affiliates, been more diligent in their approach to KM, it is likely that the current concerns would not have been so prevalent—the lack of focus on explicit knowledge, in hindsight, has not come without consequences.

Conclusion

KM exists as a hybrid of three distinct elements: people, techniques and technologies. Failure to operate in any of these areas can ultimately lead to its failure. Based on the presented case exercise, it would appear that the critical factor in achieving success is the buy-in and active participation from the people element of this trio.

Dilts and Maslow have identified that people operate across a spectrum of educational and motivational perspectives; providing technology and techniques will facilitate KM and give it every possibility of success, but people have to be fully engaged to work with that facilitation if that success is to become a reality. XIS supports this point in that the technology is adequate, and the techniques are credible and appropriate, however the people that are employed to work within this environment choose not to do so with any diligence; although educated they are not far enough up the scale to have the belief and commitment. Equally there is insufficient motivation to incentivize performance. People have become complacent that the current approach with knowledge is acceptable.

The migration of XIS activities to XET's IS function has highlighted the extent to which the current XIS KM culture is flawed. My concern is that with much of the XET's IS senior management team being positioned from XIS, this culture will persist. Once the current crisis is averted it remains to be seen if knowledge apathy will prevail. To sustain success KM requires a senior management sponsor, somebody that themselves has the educational and motivational maturity to persist in the pursuit of successful KM.

Case Exercise References

Ackoff, R.L. (1989) From Data to Wisdom, *Journal of Applied Systems Analysis* 16: 3–9.

Bali, R.K. (2008a) Working Smarter with KM, Lecture 3: M34SOR, Coventry University.

Bali, R.K. (2008b) Introduction to KM, Lecture 1: M34SOR, Coventry University.

Bateson, G. (1972) *Steps to an Ecology of Mind.* New York: Ballantine Books.

Bhatt, G.D. (2001) Knowledge Management in Organizations: Examining the Interaction Between Technologies, Techniques and People, *Journal of Knowledge Management*, 5(1): 68–75.

Blackler, F. (1995) Knowledge, Knowledge Work and Organizations: An Overview and Interpretation, *Organization Studies*, 16(6): 1021–1047.

Committee on Human Factors, National Research Council (1987) Human Factors in Automated and Robotic Space Systems: Proceedings of a Symposium. Washington, DC: Commission on Behavioral and Social Sciences and Education.

Dilts, R.B. (1996) *Visionary Leadership Skills: Creating a World to Which People Want to Belong*. Capitola, CA: Meta Publications.

Emery, F.E. (1959) Characteristics of Socio-Technical Systems, Document No. 257, Tavistock Institute of Human Relations, London.

Glasser, P. (1998) The Knowledge Factor, *CIO* magazine, December 15: 1–9.

Grant, K.A. (2007) Tacit Knowledge Revisited—We Can Still Learn from Polanyi. *The Electronic Journal of Knowledge Management*, 5(2) 173–180. Available online at www.ejkm.com.

Kane, H., Ragsdell, G., and Oppenheim, C. (2006) Knowledge Management Methodologies, *The Electronic Journal of Knowledge Management*, 4(2): 141–152.

Kropotkin, P. (1902) *Mutual Aid: A Factor of Evolution* (Reprinted 2005). Boston, MA: Porter Sargent Publishers.

Machlup, F. (1980) *Knowledge: Its Creation, Distribution, and Economic Significance*. Princeton, NJ: Princeton University Press.

Marakas, G.M. (1999) *Decision Support Systems in the Twenty-First Century*. Englewood Cliffs, NJ: Prentice-Hall.

Maslow, A.H. (1954) *Motivation and Personality*. New York: Harper & Row.

Nelson, B. (1994) *1001 Ways to Reward Employees*. New York: Workman Publishing.

OED (2008) *Oxford English Dictionary*. Available online at www.askoxford.com/concise_oed/knowledge? view=uk (accessed March 16, 2008).

Polanyi, M. (1966) *The Tacit Dimension*. New York: Doubleday.

Polanyi, M. (1967) *The Tacit Dimension*. New York: Anchor Books.

Shieh-Chieh, F., Fu-Sheng, T., and Kuo-Chien, C. (2005) Knowledge Sharing Routines, Task Efficiency and Team Service Quality in Instant Service-Giving Settings, *Journal of American Academy of Business*, 6(1).

Shariq, S.Z. (1997) Knowledge Management: An Emerging Discipline, *Journal of Knowledge Management*, 1(1): 75–82.

Sharp, P.J. (2003) MaKE: A Knowledge Management Method, unpublished Ph.D. thesis, Staffordshire University.

Skyrme, D. and Amidon, D. (1997) The Knowledge Agenda, *Journal of Knowledge Management*, 1(1): 27–37.

Trist, E.L. (1981) The Evolution of Socio-Technical Systems: A Conceptual Framework and Action Research Program, Occasional paper No. 2, Ontario Quality of Working Life Centre, Ontario.

Weber, R. (2007) Addressing Failure Factors in Knowledge Management, *Journal of Knowledge Management*, 5(3): 333–346.

Wiig, K.M. (1997) Knowledge Management: An Introduction and Perspective, *Journal of Knowledge Management*, 1(1): 6–14.

Case Exercise Questions

1 How did Company X attempt to organize its knowledge?

2 Are the intelligence gathering processes sufficient?

3 What should be done next?

4 What are the major lessons learnt from this case exercise?

FURTHER READING

Bali, R.K. (Ed.) (2005) *Clinical Knowledge Management: Opportunities and Challenges.* Hershey, PA: Idea Group Publishing.

Jackson., M. (2000) *Systems Approaches to Management.* New York: Kluwer Academic/Plenum Publishers.

Lehaney, B., Clarke, S., Coakes, E., and Jack, G. (2004) *Beyond Knowledge Management.* Hershey, PA: Idea Group Publishing.

REFERENCES

Ackoff, R.L. (1979) The Future of Operational Research is Past, *Journal of the Operational Research Society,* 30(3): 189–199.

Banathy, B. (1996) *Designing Social Systems in a Changing World.* New York: Plenum.

Bertalanffy, L. von (1968) *General System Theory: Foundations, Development, Applications.* Revised edition. New York: George Braziller.

Boddy D. and Buchanan, D. (1992) *The Expertise of the Change Agent.* London: Prentice-Hall.

Burrell G. and Morgan G. (1979) *Sociological Paradigms and Organizational Analysis.* London: Heinemann.

Checkland, P.B. (1981 and 1993) *Systems Thinking, Systems Practice.* Chichester: Wiley.

Checkland, P.B. and Scholes, J. (1990) *Soft Systems Methodology in Action.* Chichester: Wiley.

Churchman, C. (1967) Wicked Problems, *Management Science,* 14: 141–142.

Greenberger, M., Crenson, M., and Crissey, B. (1976) *Models in the Policy Process.* New York: Russell Sage.

Habermas, J. (1972) *Knowledge and Human Interests.* Boston, MA: Beacon Press.

Jackson, M. (1992) *Systems Methodology for the Management Sciences.* London: Plenum.

Jackson, M. (1993) *Beyond the Fads: Systems Thinking for Managers.* Centre for Systems Studies Working Paper Number 3. University of Hull.

Jackson, M. (2000) *Systems Approaches to Management.* New York: Kluwer Academic/Plenum Publishers.

Johnson, G., Langley, A., Melin, L., and Whittington, R. (2007) *Strategy as Practice: Research Directions and Resources.* Cambridge: Cambridge University Press.

Lehaney, B., Warwick, S., and Wisniewski, M. (1994) The Use of Quantitative Modeling Methods in the UK: Some National and Regional Comparisons, *Journal of European Business Education,* 3(2): 57–71.

Lehaney, B., Clarke, S., and Paul, R.J. (1999) A Case of an Intervention in an Outpatients Department, *Journal of the Operational Research Society,* 50(9): 877–891.

Lehaney, B., Clarke, S., Coakes, E., and Jack, G. (2004) *Beyond Knowledge Management.* Hershey, PA: Idea Group Publishing.

Lewis, P. (1994) *Information-Systems Development.* London: Pitman.

Mingers, J. (1984) Subjectivism and Soft Systems Methodology—A Critique. *Journal of Applied Systems Analysis,* 11: 85–103.

Mingers, J. and Taylor, S. (1992) The Use of Soft Systems Methodology in Practice, *Journal of the Operational Research Society,* 43(4): 321–322.

Prince User Group, Binder Hamlyn (1993) *Report of the Inquiry into the London Ambulance Service.* London: Prince User Group, Binder Hamlyn.

Rosenhead, J. (Ed.) (1989) *Rational Analysis for a Problematic World*. Chichester: Wiley.

Sackman, H. (1967) *Computers, Systems Science and Evolving Society: The Challenge of Man-Machine Digital Systems*. New York: Wiley.

Taylor, F. (1911) *The Principles of Scientific Management*. New York: Harper Bros.

Ulrich, W. (1983) *Critical Heuristics of Social Planning: A New Approach to Practical Philosophy*. Berne: Haupt.

Ulrich, W. (1987) Critical Heuristics of Social Systems Design, *European Journal of Operational Research*, 31(3): 276–283.

Wilson, B. (1984) *Systems: Concepts, Methodologies, and Applications*. Chichester: Wiley.

Chapter 5

Knowledge: The Organization, Culture and Learning

INTRODUCTION

This chapter will introduce key organizational concepts (e.g. organizational structures, the learning organization, organizational culture and organizational change) and discuss how these essential components relate to effective KM implementation. This will be followed by a discussion of the benefits offered to companies introducing KM into their organizations, as well as the socio-technical perspectives on KM. The application to, and impact on, contemporary businesses will be described (and illustrated by way of case studies).

THE LEARNING ORGANIZATION

The concept of the learning organization (LO) is said to have been coined by Chris Argyris (a Harvard-based academic) but seems to have been popularized by the seminal work of Peter Senge (and his book *The Fifth Discipline*, first published in 1990). We should emphasize that, although closely linked, the terms "learning organization" and "organizational learning" are not the same. The overlap occurs because organizational learning is a prerequisite for a learning organization.

Senge (1992) describes learning organizations as places "where people continually expand their capacity to create the results they truly desire, where new and expansive patterns of thinking are nurtured, where collective aspiration is set free, and where people are continually learning to see the whole (reality) together." Pedler *et al.* (1991) agree with this viewpoint, stating that ". . . a Learning Company is an organization that facilitates the learning of all its members and continually transforms itself."

A learning organization is essentially one where the objectives and the company are one and the same. The organization encourages learning and sharing and dissemination of information and knowledge (and an appropriate infrastructure is in place to ensure this). New ideas, and change associated with them, are achieved by way of shared vision. The organization's culture is central to any change process and this is discussed in detail later in this chapter.

The LO is in a position to continuously transform itself (perhaps because of external pressures or even internal efficiency and effectiveness) and has the freedom to let go of the past and attempt novel, innovative ways forward to achieve this. The LO is a unique organization inasmuch that both successes and failures are examined for their potential for learning; there is very much an "anti blame" culture in place as mistakes are permitted (in the very best LOs, mistakes may even be encouraged for their learning potential and value). It could be argued in fact that without trying new ideas, and an element of trial and error, true innovation is not possible. The following table summarizes the four levels of learning.

Senge describes five disciplines as being essential and conducive to learning and engagement, allowing organizational actors to become active participants in the learning (and associated change) process. The five components are:

Personal Mastery

This component refers to the ability and discipline of an individual to clarify and deepen his/her personal vision. By doing so, energy can be focused, hopefully allowing the individual to view things in an objective manner. Clarity is of paramount importance here, as is the constant technique of checking/re-checking where one currently is towards attaining the vision. By way of a simple analogy, is an individual embarks on a personal and professional development (career) plan, goals should be set which are both ambitious and realistic. Milestones should also be incorporated that allow the individual to check on progress and, if necessary, to reappraise or even add or amend additional goals and milestones.

Team Learning

This component aims to align and developing the capacity of a team to create the results they desire. It is a truism that people (actors) within an organization require the ability to work well with one another in order to, collectively, achieve organizational goals. This process may

Table 5.1 *Levels of Learning According to David Skyrme Associates (2008)*

Level 1	*Learning facts, knowledge, processes and procedures* Applies to known situations where changes are minor
Level 2	*Learning new job skills that are transferable to other situations* Applies to new situations where existing responses need to be changed. Bringing in outside expertise is a useful tool here
Level 3	*Learning to adapt* Applies to more dynamic situations where the solutions need developing Experimentation, and deriving lessons from success and failure is the mode of learning here
Level 4	*Learning to learn* Is about innovation and creativity; designing the future rather than merely adapting to it. This is where assumptions are challenged and knowledge is reframed

start with actions as simple as brainstorming (or mindstorming), suspending personal assumptions and working together "as one."

Shared Vision

This component focuses on the ability of a group to perceive and rely upon a common viewpoint of a desired future. This aspect provides the focus and energy of learning that reflects both individual (personal) and organizational goals and visions. If carried out correctly, this component tries to align both personal and organizational goals; individuals strive to learn and the positive culture within the organization is highly conducive to enable this.

Mental Models

Senge describes mental models as assumptions that influence how individuals perceive and influence the world and, as a consequence, how we choose to take action. The value of mental images comes when individuals compare new ideas with their (internal) perception of how the world works; if these new ideas are significantly at odds with the mental images (perception), this can prevent them from being turned into reality.

Systems Thinking

Very much at the heart of Senge's thinking comes Systems Thinking. Having acknowledged that organizations are inherently complex entities with various and varied key components, the approach attempts to understand how these components interact with each other and how these interactions affect the organization. In order to function correctly, the approach requires managers to think from a systems perspective and thus also have a long-term perspective. More detail on systems thinking and its importance to KM can be found later in the book.

THE IMPORTANCE OF ORGANIZATIONAL CULTURE

The term *culture* can be used in a variety of contexts. For example, we can describe a person as cultured when (s)he comes to appreciate fine art or literature; on a biological level, cells can be grown in cultures or we describe a country's culture (those national characteristics indigenous to that country).

Definitions of culture are notoriously widespread. The difficulty in refining to a single definition is exacerbated when it is considered that, according to the anthropologists Kroeber and Kluckhohn (1952), over 150 different definitions of the term "culture" have been formed. Little wonder then, that confusion over the accepted definition of culture exists.

Smircich (1983) suggests that the plethora of definitions can be readily explained by the fact that the entire concept of culture has been extrapolated from the area of anthropology where there is "no consensus of meaning" (Smircich, 1983: 339–58). Brown (1995) cites

Edward B. Tylor's (1871) definition of culture as "the complex whole which includes knowledge, beliefs, art, morals, law, custom . . . acquired by man" (Tylor, 1871: 3).

Pheysey (1993) suggests that culture is "a way of seeing that is common to many people" (p. 3). Perhaps the most cited definition of culture is that of Geert Hofstede (1994), a leading academic and consultant in organizational anthropology and international management. Based in the Netherlands, and the founding director of the Institute for Research on Intercultural Cooperation (IRIC), Hofstede's professional career has spanned foreman, plant manager and chief psychologist on the international staff of IBM. In his book *Cultures and Organizations*, Hofstede analogizes organizational culture as the "software of the mind" and suggests that culture can be thought of as the ". . . collective programming of the human mind that distinguishes the members of one human group from those of another" (Hofstede, 1994: 5).

In simple terms, describe organizational culture as "an attitude which governs the way things are done in an organization," closely aping the viewpoint of Bower (1966) who describes culture as "the way things are done around here." Hofstede (1994: 4) further states that each person carries patterns of thinking and feeling that stay with them throughout their life. Acquired and learnt during childhood, when the person is most open to learning, assimilation and dissemination of information, these patterns gradually become entrenched within the persona.

Figure 5.1 (Hofstede, 1994: 6) depicts the distinction between human nature on one side and an individual's personality on the other side. When learning something else, the established patterns must be *unlearnt*, which Hofstede (1994) says is inherently more difficult (perhaps a case of old habits dying hard?). Following on from this, Hofstede (1994) puts forward the idea that all countries possess a factor called *management*, its meaning changing from one country to another. In order to understand its processes and problems, historical and cultural insights into local phenomena are taken into account.

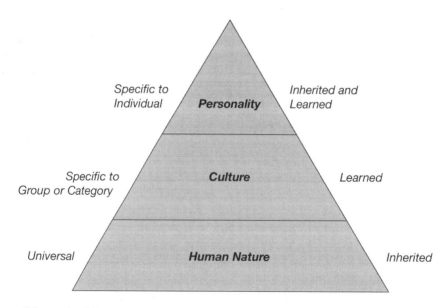

Figure 5.1 *Levels of Mental Programming.*
Source: Hofstede (1994: 6)

Table 5.2 *Kroeber and Kluckhohn's Cultural Traits*

Culture can be shared	by individuals in families or by individuals in society
Culture is learned	by the acquisition and transmission of teachings and experience
Culture is transgenerational	and is passed from one generation to another
Culture is influenced by perception	in the shaping of mannerisms, behavior and provides the structure to how a person regards their environment
Culture is adaptive	and is based on a person's ability to change or adapt

In yet another of his works, Hofstede (1993) has suggested that universal management theories are non-existent and vary according to the country in which they are applied. It may seem that we have over-examined Hofstede's work but we would argue that this only serves to reinforce its importance. Indeed, such is its acceptance that various authors agree that his work ". . . has had a major influence on how we think about the culture of organizations in different countries" (Brown, 1995: 46).

Various studies (Pennings, 1993; Thornhill, 1993; Vitell *et al.*, 1993) use Hofstede's various contributions to explain the effects of culture on decision making, executive award systems and training regimens respectively. But how exactly can culture be measured? According to Kroeber and Kluckhohn (1952), culture possesses the following traits.

ORGANIZATIONAL CULTURE

Much like trying to pinpoint a single definition of culture, defining and classifying *organization* is equally difficult and opinion is divided. Robbins (1991) suggests that an organization is a systematic arrangement of people who come together to achieve a common purpose, while Hutchison and Rosenberg (1994) argue that the issue is clouded as the definition changes depending on "who is asking and why they are interested" (p. 101). March and Simon (1958) concur, adding that it is substantially easier to give examples of formal organizations than to pinpoint a universally-accepted and formal definition. It would, however, still be beneficial to attempt, for the purposes of this book, an "uncontroversial" definition of organization.

We would therefore support the view that an organization is a ". . . social arrangement for the controlled performance of collective goals" (Huczynski and Buchanan, 1991: 1). According to Gibson *et al.* (1994), in order to animate the organization, *processes* (such as communications and decision-making) and *structures* (formalized patterns of how its people and jobs are grouped) are used. Extending the notion of culture into an organization leads us to the definition of *organizational culture*. Schein (1990) highlights the pattern of basic assumptions used by individuals and groups to deal with an organization's personality and *feel,* which forms the basis of that organization's culture.

A biography of Richard Branson (Jackson, 1995) profiles the conception and growth of the *Virgin* brand. Great insight is provided into Branson's corporate philosophy with Branson himself attributing his personal and corporate success to the organizational culture present. Jackson (ibid.: 303) summarizes the *Virgin* culture as one where ". . . it was idle to ask whether something could be done. Virgin people would assume that it could, and confine themselves to asking how."

Some examples (the list is not exhaustive) of indexes that can combine to form the basis of an organization's culture include reports, letters, memos, emails, health and safety regulations, and rulebooks (Bali, 1999). Some examples of protocols of a more-verbalized nature are given: forms of addresses, repeated stories/myths, "in"-jokes, rumors and speculation. Factors such as dressing styles/requirements and *de rigueur* career paths are cited as additional factors that can contribute to and act as a measure of an organization's culture.

It is this same organizational culture that defines behavior and which motivates its individuals and affects the way that the organization processes information. Many researchers and authors (among them Gummesson, 1988 and Gibson *et al.*, 1994) compare organizations to an iceberg. According to Gummesson (1988), an iceberg only shows 10–15 percent of its total mass above the surface water and the iceberg is thus a valid and appropriate model to show the visible and non-visible facets to an organization's culture. We would submit that this conceptualization upholds the importance of deeper research into an organization in order to gain access to the "hidden" 85–90 percent of the organization's value and belief system.

Academic studies and consultancy projects in the U.K., Europe and the U.S. have been carried out by Hampden-Turner (1990) in order to better understand the nature of organizational culture. Hampden-Turner, educated both in the U.K. and the U.S., regularly lectures on the topic throughout the world and is in a position to comment on different cultural attitudes between countries. He suggests that the concept of organizational culture can also be compared to the notion of Rorschach inkblots (used in psychology), where a patient is asked to describe what (s)he "sees."

We would offer the suggestion that shared thoughts, ideals and procedures all contribute to forming a company's culture. The culture of some Japanese-owned car manufacturers, such as Nissan and Honda, starting their day with cross-plant exercises in the yard serves as a suitable example. It should be remembered, however, that the Japanese, as opposed to the British or the Americans, live in quite different environments in anthropological and commercial terms. Initially in the U.K., cross-plant exercises must have seemed alien to the workers but, as suggested by Fiedler *et al.* (1994), the feeling of togetherness and bonding has combined to overcome any awkwardness to make this "norm" work in the U.K.-based plants.

The prevailing patterns of behavior that form a company culture are generally less explicit than formal rules and procedures. Nevertheless, these patterns can often be a powerful influence on the way that employees and managers approach commercial objectives, be they profit maximization or customer care. Robbins (1991) identifies organizational culture as being a mix of ten key characteristics.

Additionally, company cultures can have either a positive (helping productivity) or negative (hindering productivity) effect. Increasingly, greater importance has been attached to improving or, in some cases, creating a corporate culture. While there is nothing inherently incorrect with Robbins' "ten-point" approach, it is our contention that this approach is too formal and regimented in its outlook. We believe that a "softer" approach would be beneficial in the interests of clarity and understanding and agree with the "alternative" characteristics cited by Williams *et al.* (1993) (a group of U.K. researchers who were commissioned to write a book by the

Table 5.3 *Robbins' Ten Characteristics*

Individual initiative	describing the degree of freedom, flexibility and responsibility an individual has
Integration	or the extent to which units within the organization are encouraged to operate in a co-ordinated manner
Control	deals with the rules and regulations that govern an individual's working day
Risk tolerance	describing the extent to which individuals are encouraged in terms of innovation and aggression
Direction	describing the extent to which an organization develops clear objectives for staff to follow
Reward systems	including the degree to which factors such as salary increases are based on employee performance criteria
Communication patterns	deal with the way an organization's communications are related to the management structure
Conflict tolerance	details whether individuals are encouraged to air (and hopefully resolve) grievances freely
Management support	includes the extent to which management provide clear channels of communication
Identity	takes into account the way in which individuals identify with and "fit in" to the organization, rather than their own (often narrow) sphere of experience

Institute of Personnel Management with the aim of shedding light on the U.K. experience of cultural change), who argue that:

■ *Culture is learnt*—environmental conditions are the foundations for individual's beliefs, attitudes and values, which in turn dictate the culture of the organization. Both internal (the socio-technical facets of the organization, encompassing the internal mechanisms such as planning, control, technology, decision-making processes and training) and external (factors such as economic, legislative and technological influences) organizational environments can affect organizational culture.

■ *Culture is both an input and an output*—influenced by the socio-technical systems of the organization, organizational culture is the result of actions and elements of future action, best depicted by Figure 5.2 (from Williams *et al.*, 1993).

Figure 5.2 shows that organizational culture is influenced by the socio-technical systems of the organization, which are in turn influenced by the common beliefs, attitudes and values of its members. The procedures adopted by management create the work environment for the other members of the organization. If managers have been members of the organization for some time, they themselves can be a product of the culture. Hence their strategies and procedures have, almost inevitably, been conditioned by the culture. Given that culture is both an input and output, it is likely that this attitude is both self-perpetuating and highly resistant to change.

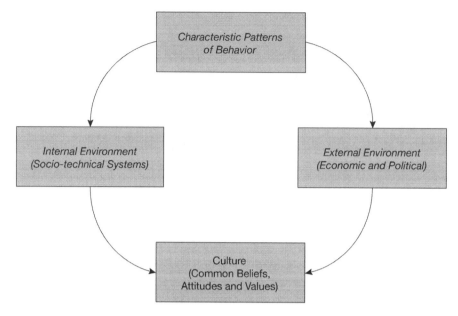

Figure 5.2 *Culture as Both an Input and an Output.*
Source: Williams *et al.* (1993: 16)

Culture is partly unconscious—commonly held beliefs are unconscious on two levels. First, members unconsciously process information that influences the way in which they think. Second, the conscious beliefs, attitudes and values that underlie behavior may repeatedly lead to success to the extent that they are taken for granted.

Culture is historically based—organizations are based on the assumptions and structures of their original founders. Once a particular business direction has been decided upon, successive management generations are often tied to the inherent structures and organizational assumptions that have been set. The original beliefs, attitudes and values (that make up the original organizational culture) may influence successive management generations as organizational decisions are made within the context of the pre-existing culture.

Culture is commonly-held—culture, on an organizational and societal level, can be shared, as different individuals would be affiliated to groups containing similarly like-minded individuals. For example, an organization spread over many sites may comprise individuals who possess common attitudes, thoughts and behavior, despite being separated geographically.

Culture is heterogeneous—in reality, beliefs, attitudes and values are common to work groups, departments, organizations and society. Hence, culture can be common between individuals in a marketing department of a large organization but this culture may not be shared with, perhaps, the IT department (who would possess their own, distinct, set of beliefs, attitudes and values). The existence of sub-cultures can be beneficial if a department's culture results in increased focus on their aims and objectives. Conversely, sub-cultures can also have a detrimental effect if common co-ordination over the organization is limited.

In order to depict the manifestation of culture at different levels in an organization, Hofstede (1994) developed the concept of the "Cultural Onion." For the purposes of this book, we have adapted the diagram (Figure 5.3) to also include organizational structures.

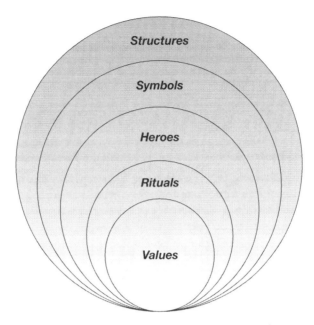

Figure 5.3 *The Cultural Onion.*
Source: adapted from Hofstede (1994)

Referring to Figure 5.3 (and paraphrasing Hofstede's (1994) thoughts), at the heart of the cultural onion is the organization's core *values* (beliefs that hold and guide the organization's progress). Surrounding this layer is the *ritual* layer (for example, the organization's approach to employee relations or the tendency to arrange office parties). The next layer is *heroes* and describes the individuals in the organization and their respective competencies and behaviors. This layer is surrounded by *symbols* (the outward signs of the organization, for example, the corporate image). The final layer, *structures*, encases the inner layers and is the control and guidance mechanism of the firm, which dictates how the organization's activities are planned and co-ordinated.

After analyzing the various layers to the diagram, it is our contention that organizational change consultants (and researchers) try to change and influence the outer layer (structure) and make little inroads into the deeper layers of the "onion." To paraphrase the thoughts of an anonymous author on the Internet (Anon, 1997), we would urge caution when attempting to change organizations as *real* change has to cut right through to the core of the onion, which, like the vegetable, often leads to tears.

The manifestation of culture at different levels in an organization leads us to define *management*. Authors such as Earl (1989) and Mintzberg (1989) present management as a generic term that describes how different activities are completed efficiently with and through other people. This notion is extended by breaking down management into the four distinct functions of *planning* (the definition of goals, strategy establishment), *organizing* (which tasks are to be done by whom and reporting structures), *leading* (motivation of employees, conflict resolution) and *controlling* (monitoring activities ensuring fulfillment to prior objectives). As U.K. organizations become increasingly oriented towards a European, if not global, market, the significance of cultural understanding becomes increasingly important. Dudley (1990) puts forward the notion that an organization that fails to reflect the changing needs and requirements of a (global) market will fail in its attempt to re-focus any competitive edge it may already have. Hence, competitively, it will be outperformed.

Having given definitions for culture, organization and organizational culture, we can now apply these aspects to the structures of an organization. Harrison's (1972) framework consists of four cultural types and is used as a basis for comparison between organizational cultures. The four cultural approaches (termed orientations) are:

- *Power*—demonstrated by power-hungry and power-motivated organizations who seek to dominate their environment. These organizations treat individuals, departments and other companies as commodities, with no real regard for personal feeling.
- *Role*—generally equate to bureaucratic organizations, where strict adherence to rigid procedures is the norm. In this type of organization, status and titles are important.
- *Task*—is where structures and actions are judged by their contribution to the main organizational objectives. Executing these aims successfully is of paramount importance.
- *People*—where employees are regarded as the organization's most important asset. Action by consensus of opinion is normal. Staff welfare, personal and professional development are key facets.

After analysis of Harrison's (1972) typologies, we would simplify his orientations by typifying *power cultures* as those whose managerial stance is "do as I say," *role cultures* as those whose management attitude is "rules and regulations are King," *task cultures* as those whose managerial style is "teamwork gets the job done" and *people cultures* as those whose managerial stance is "people first."

Carnall (1995) carried out studies in the U.K. and focused on change on three levels: (1) *Psychological*, identifying the attitudes and skills needed to be an effective change leader; (2) *Managerial*, detailing how managers plan the change process to help ensure implementations without setbacks; and (3) *Strategic*, showing how change must be managed as part of a coherent strategic plan. Carnall (1995) broadly suggests that there are six model structures:

1 *Entrepreneurial structure*—a relatively simple model where everything depends on the owner of the business who makes all decisions. Other employees are taken on to carry out specific tasks but, because of little or no departmental structuring, this actually increases the organization's flexibility.
2 *Functional structure*—where an organization is split into distinct activities (such as marketing, legal, IT) and co-ordination takes place by a board of directors, overseen by a managing director.
3 *Product structure*—building on the precepts of a functional structure, the product structure makes individuals responsible for particular products and services. A group is allocated responsibility for particular products or range of products and/or services and are allocated specialists from disciplines such as marketing, legal and engineering. In this manner, these product groups are better equipped to respond to the demands of the market.
4 *Divisional structure*—as an organization increases in size, senior management become less concerned with the day-to-day operations, preferring to concentrate on medium to long-term strategies. Dividing the company into autonomous divisions means that everyday

decisions are carried out by each separate division, perhaps concentrating on products or markets. Each division often has management committees which would then report to the organization's senior management. The divisional structure means that considerations regarding costs and profit are left to the committees of the autonomous divisions, leaving Senior Management to concentrate on other matters. Accountability and responsibility is "pushed down" through the organization.

5 *Matrix structure*—are often found when an organization deals with more than one project at a time, calling for various co-ordination skills. As projects may be medium to long-term, this would require the co-ordination of projects, in terms of specialist knowledge and the timely deployment of necessary resources. Matrix structures enable the effective development of specialists who are working towards the objectives of a project while providing a base for the flexible use of these professionals.

6 *Federal structure*—building on the foundations of the divisional structure, distinct business units are introduced. Each unit has autonomous responsibility over its product market without resort to a divisional structure. Federal structures allow for clear accountability and ensures that the bulk of resources is not expended at divisional level.

There is common agreement (Harrison, 1972; Handy, 1985; Robbins, 1991; Pheysey, 1993; Carnall, 1995) that organizational model structures and cultural orientations are not mutually-exclusive and can be integrated with one another depending on the circumstance, the culture in force and the management *in situ* at an organization.

SOCIO-TECHNICAL ISSUES

The Impact of Technology

A diagram from Williams *et al.* (1993), reproduced in Figure 5.4, shows the major determinants of culture and illustrates that culture (the common attitudes, beliefs and values) results from the external environment, the systems, structure and technology of the organization and from the behavior of the work group. The external environment impacts on the organization's cultural behavior as variations such as legislation and politics place varying demands on the organization. This has an influence on the strategy of the organization and the systems and technology that are implemented. The recruitment of persons from a wide-ranging social, cultural and educational background will result in idiosyncratic behavior when these persons are placed in the organization.

Hofstede (1994) explains how the technology of an organization can impact on culture in terms of the *boundaries* of an organization, the degree of *differentiation* and *integration* of the technology. As Wiseman (1985) tells us, the changing nature of IT over the years has resulted in three distinct conceptual models of IT (namely Data Processing, Management Information Systems and Strategic Information Systems), each model having a different effect on the organization–technology relationship.

Apart from Zmud (1984), there appears to be little evidence of research into the cultural aspects of the Business–Technology boundary of an organization. From Ward and Peppard

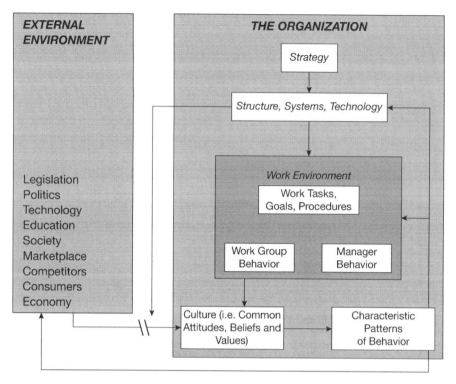

Figure 5.4 *Culture—The Organization and the External Environment.*

Source: Williams *et al.* (1993)

(1995) we find a reference to an article in the *EDP Analyzer* Organizing for the 1990s, which discusses the merits and demerits of various organizational structures and the varying skills required by IT managers. Little mention is made of the close relationship necessary between IT and business objectives. They go on to argue that Johnson's (1992) *Cultural Web* (reproduced in Figure 5.5) offers great insight to understanding the cultural aspects of the IT–Business relationship.

Figure 5.5, *The Cultural Web*, apes closely the reasoning behind the earlier diagram of *The Cultural Onion* and takes the view that while individuals in an organization may hold distinct attitudes, beliefs and values from their colleagues, each set of attitudes, beliefs and values is nevertheless held at the core of the organization (the Paradigm circle in the *Cultural Web*).

Ward and Peppard (1995) go on to suggest that the IT and business aspects to a business are two distinct paradigms and, furthermore, because of these respective paradigms: ". . . each creates a relatively homogeneous approach to the interpretation of the complexity that the organization faces" (p. 18). The perception of Johnson (1992) is that the paradigm (in our case, either the Business or IT paradigm) is surrounded by six components through which core attitudes, beliefs and values are communicated:

1 *Stories and Myths*—almost part of an organization's folklore and includes tales that employees relate to new employees warning them of past failures/consequences and the fate of maverick recruits.

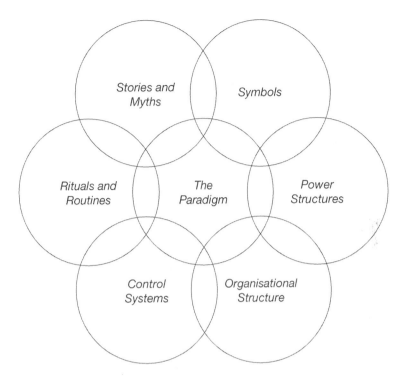

Figure 5.5 *The Cultural Web.*
Source: Johnson (1992)

2 *Symbols*—includes such aspects as dress codes, job titles, executives' cars and *de rigueur* attitudes such as addressing directors as "Sir."
3 *Rituals and Routines*—range from director's signing requisitions to required attendance at weekly board meetings. No real business advantage may be gained by carrying out these duties, but they all encompass rituals that may have historical relevance to the organization.
4 *Control Systems*—pay and reward systems and the managerial hierarchy serve as examples of control systems which monitor performance.
5 *Organizational Structures*—hierarchical structures and product or service-based business units are examples of organizational structures. This includes the position of the IT organization relative to the position of the Business organization.
6 *Power Structures*—are often an indicator of where the major organizational influence is and is often the main target for any change programs. A common difficulty is when the main personnel targets for change are also those who hold the power.

The growth of IT, and society's increasing dependence upon it, has been both prolific and extensive. As more and more technology found, and continues to find, its way into the commercial environment, several researchers (Bessant and Cole, 1985; Johnston and Vitale, 1988; Laver, 1989; Boddy and Gunson, 1996) confirmed that organizational structures and cultures altered to reflect the changing circumstances and to exploit the competitive advantages from increased efficiency and effectiveness.

The technical steps have been summarized in various sources (e.g. Bali, 1999) in order to highlight the major developments that have taken place in computing. This historical perspective is useful for providing insights into the *causes* behind technical changes and also the *effects* of the changes, in organizational and commercial terms, brought about. Additionally, the question of whether these developments were as a result of direct pressure from increasingly complex business environments, for example, managers wanting more pertinent information, has been included.

New methodological and business processes have necessitated the use of new and novel ways of working. Human attitudes to the new computing technology (Human Computer Interaction—HCI) have been of prime importance. The position occupied by technology in organizations throughout the years has depended on the commercial aspirations of the organization and also the industry in which the organization operated. The review has shown that computers have been used to facilitate and disseminate innovation in organizations. A simplistic SWOT (Strengths, Weaknesses, Opportunities, Threats) analysis would reveal the benefits, together with relative weaknesses, of IT at each key chronological stage outlined.

Some of the more major evolutionary steps of IT took place in the 1950s, with the U.S. leading the global transformation from the industrial to the information age. The acceptability, however, of the ongoing changes was far from unanimous. A study conducted at that time by Garrity and Barnes (1968) indicated that only nine out of twenty-seven installations surveyed covered their initial operating costs. However, progress was being made on other aspects of the new technology and as cost, performance and potential usage of the technology improved, acceptability began to replace the initial skepticism. According to Schultheis and Sumner (1995), IT implementations in organizations occur for the following reasons (either individually or in combination):

- To improve efficiency—the execution of tasks *correctly*. Generally this refers to the automation of routine paper-based tasks. An example would be using IT to process hundreds of works orders per day.
- To improve effectiveness—executing the *right* tasks. Using a computer database to select likely prospects for a marketing campaign would be an example of using IT effectively.
- To bring about transformation—changing the *manner* in which the business is executed. By way of example, diversifying the business, via the strategic use of IT, to provide goods or services distinct to those originally provided.

Mintzberg (1989) set out to order the literature on organizational structuring and to extract its key messages and to synthesize these into an integrated picture of the structuring of organizations. According to him, an organization's structure consists of a highly specialized and skilled operating core, taking the form of individuals under a professional and regulatory body, confirmed by Handy (1985). Anthony (1965) substantiates by offering several schematics depicting the three kinds of activity of an organization, together with the typical managerial layers and functions affected:

- *Operational planning* (the day-to-day activities of the organization and where first-line managers collect data, results and events).

Figure 5.6 *Activities and Framework for an Organization's IS Requirements.*
Source: adapted from Anthony (1965)

- *Tactical planning* (where operational activities are reviewed and appraised by middle managers in order to ensure their adherence to pre-set targets and goals).
- *Strategic planning* (usually carried out by the top layer of management, where data and information from the operational and tactical planning stages is used to set the organization's long-term agenda).

For reasons of brevity and clarity, we have adapted and combined two of his diagrams, as shown in Figure 5.6. This diagram shows the need for computer-based, pertinent information systems that would be of strategic interest to managers, particularly in the form of Management Information Systems (MIS). As Schultheis and Sumner (1995) explain, the fast-moving strategies in modern organizations leading to the increasing needs of IT have clouded the area of MIS to the extent where, as Lucey (1991) says, there is ". . . no universally accepted definition of a MIS and those that exist reflect the emphasis of the particular writer" (p. 1).

Despite this, Lucey (1991) attempts to put forward a definition of a Management Information System as an ". . . integrated structure of databases and information flows over all levels and components of an organization whereby the collection, transfer and presentation of information is optimized to meet the needs of the organization" (p. 2); while Long (1989) is of the opinion that a MIS is more of a ". . . system to convert data from internal and external sources into information and to communicate that information . . . to managers at all levels in all functions to enable them to make timely and effective decisions" (p. 547).

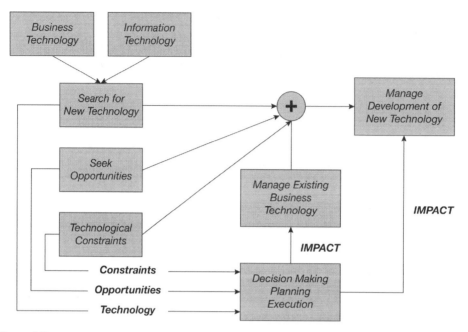

Figure 5.7 *The Integration of MIS and Management.*
Source: Lucas (1990)

For the purposes of this book, we have decided to put forward, as an acceptable definition of a MIS, the most contemporary description as given by Licker (1997): ". . . an integrated user + machine system that provides information to support operations, management analysis and decision-making functions in an organization" (p. 5).

The integration of IT, Management Information Systems, information flows and management is best typified by the schematic (Figure 5.7) given by Lucas (1990). Although we would agree with all of the definitions given in this section, we would suggest that, in a commercial environment (and for the layman), the purpose of IT for organizations is to provide the *right* information at the *right* time. It should be noted that this is particularly relevant for KM-based initiatives. The "value-chain," dividing an organization into *value activities* (distinct activities—such as order processing, advertising, marketing—necessary in order to carry out day-to-day business), confirms our current, and increasing, reliance on information.

However, Scott-Morton (1995) reports that Information Systems only became computer-based after the accepted advent of IT systems. Before this, information would have been paper-based, by the use of filing cabinets. Earl (1989) confirms the organization-wide impact and importance of IT given the increasing importance of the information created and used (Porter, 1985) by that organization. This ties in with the inherent structure of the organization in question.

EVOLUTION OF KNOWLEDGE MANAGEMENT SYSTEMS

The discussions on MIS given earlier are not meant to be merely tangential. Evolution within the IT industry as well as the progression of contemporary business meant that change was,

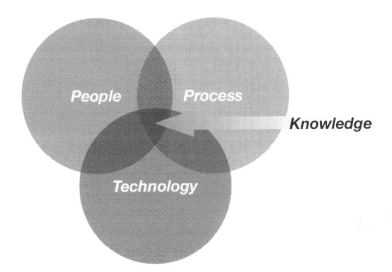

Figure 5.8 *Knowledge: Intersection of People, Process and Technology.*
Reproduced with kind permission of Doctrina Applied Research and Consulting LLC—www.consultdoctrina.com

and remains, inevitable. Some argue that KM is a relatively new form of MIS and decision making (Reference for Business, 2008) but this is a very simplistic as well as unrealistic perspective. Spender (1996) argues that confusion arises as we do not always have a clear idea of the significant differences between IT and KM. We prefer to argue the case of Gray and Meister (2003) who state that MIS differs from IT in its attention to the people and social systems into which computing systems are projected; it is this aspect that may make MIS and KM appear similar. The following schematic (provided earlier in the book) may aid understanding.

The schematic attempts to portray the importance of three essential elements for the presence of knowledge (people, process and technology). The initial arguments for the adoption of MIS followed this same logic, often necessitating cultural and organizational (process) change for successful deployment (Bali, 1999). We would submit that the schematic successfully mirrors our contemporary work environment. The socio-technical nature of contemporary human-machine interaction is evident, even during an action as simple as surfing the web. Coakes' (2002) work defines the socio-technical approach as ". . . the study of the relationships and interrelationships between the social and technical parts of any system" (p. 5).

The notion of a KMS often appears to fall between two stalls. Alavi and Leidner (2001) argue that KMS was "developed to support and enhance the organizational knowledge processes of knowledge creation, storage, retrieval, transfer and application" (p. 114). This perspective is detailed by Gupta and Sharma (2004) who state that "knowledge management systems are divided into several major categories, as follows: groupware, including e-mail, e-log and wikis; decision support systems; expert systems; document management systems; semantic networks; relational and object oriented databases; simulation tools; and artificial intelligence."

While there is nothing inherently wrong with these viewpoints, one must bear in mind that knowledge-creating activities (perhaps including creativity) "take place within and between humans" (Davenport and Prusak, 1998). Combining these opinions gives us the necessary human-centric and technology-based (socio-technical) components for our schematic.

"DOUBLE LOOP" LEARNING

We described earlier the notion and importance of the learning organization to contemporary KM initiatives. The true value of any and all knowledge that resides within, lies not through mere ownership but, rather, through effective communication and dissemination methods. After all, what use is knowledge if no one can make effective use of it?

Hence, the ability to both learn and share knowledge (within the learning organization) is of paramount importance, particularly the capability and capacity of the organization to respond to internal and external demands. Senge (1992) commented on the inextricable link between individual and entity learning by stating that:

> Organizations only learn through individuals who learn. Individual learning does not guarantee organizational learning but without it no organizational learning occurs.
>
> (Senge, 1992: 139)

If we assume that learning constantly evolves within organizations—and the true value of any worthwhile knowledge lies in its contemporary application or "freshness"—then iterative knowledge is required. When an individual learns within the organization, it is imperative that this knowledge is both retained and assimilated within the organization.

Argyris and Schön (1978) developed approaches that were intended to assist organizational learning, and they distinguished single-loop from double-loop learning. Single-loop learning involves the modification of behavior based on expectations when compared with outcomes. Double-loop learning involves the questioning of values and assumptions that led to the initial behavior. Thus, double-loop learning would be considered as critical in its nature, and it is about learning about single-loop learning. A further development is triple-loop learning (see for example Flood and Romm, 1996), in which there is learning about the learning about single-loop learning.

Learning incorporates the concepts of tacit and explicit knowledge (Polanyi, 1967). These concepts were developed by Nonaka and Takeuchi (1995) as a spiral model of organizational learning that comprises four stages. Explicit knowledge may be codified, systematic, formal and easily communicated. Tacit knowledge is personal, context specific and difficult to communicate. One of the difficulties is that our world views are not always explicit to ourselves, so communicating some of these things to others poses huge challenges. If the tacit knowledge of people within an organization can be made explicit, this is known as externalization. Such knowledge might be translated into manuals or incorporated into new products and processes. Internalization is the process of taking explicit knowledge and using it to develop tacit knowledge. Socialization is the process of sharing tacit knowledge, while combination is about the dissemination of codified knowledge. This model considers the processes as part of a continual spiral.

Managers often rely on what is known as narrative knowledge or experiential knowledge, which is to do with a history of practice within organizations. Such knowledge is invaluable, but cannot easily (if at all) be tabulated or codified in a form that would be familiar to a physical scientist, such as a chemist. There is no formula. There are guidelines and "rules of thumb," but using the same approach in a similar situation to one that had been successfully addressed previously may not achieve the same result.

Organizational learning must be more than simply adding together the learning of individuals within an organization. A learning organization extends the concept of organizational learning. While organizational learning may occur in any organization, a learning organization is one that actively supports and helps create knowledge capture and transfer. In this context, mistakes are perceived as opportunities to learn, rather than opportunities to cast blame. It is therefore interactions between individuals and the culture they create that fosters organizational learning. The more this is actively and explicitly facilitated, the more the concept of the learning organization is manifested.

Capturing individual knowledge assists in developing organizational learning. This may be by means of talking with others, publications, reports, training sessions, presentations, intranet and Internet postings, video conferencing or any other means that enables knowledge to be accessed. Ideally, knowledge needs to be organized in forms that provide ease of access and ease of understanding. It can include storage in knowledge repositories, databases and libraries. Knowledge transfer in today's digital world typically involves browsers, search engines and the use of available technology. It is important not to confuse the technology with the transfer of knowledge. The former is simply a tool in the process.

Learning to learn is key for individuals, groups and organizations. If an individual gains knowledge, it is available for their immediate use, but to share that knowledge with others and to share how the knowledge was gained, requires systematic and systemic processes to help create, capture, transfer and assess knowledge. Considering culture is vital in this, and considering technology is also helpful.

Linked to the foregoing discussions, the term "knowledge organization" is used to describe a situation in which people use systems and processes to create, manage and use knowledge-based products and services to achieve organizational goals. A knowledge organization learns from the past and adapts to sustain competitive advantage. From organizational learning, knowledge organizations have collective intelligence. Objects, data, information and knowledge are generated by knowledge workers, with content captured, organized and stored, preserved to enable its reuse and leveraging by people and groups other than those who generated it.

This requires an infrastructure to enable sharing of content across all elements of an organization and even with customers and suppliers. In addition, process needs to exist to integrate content from multiple sources and utilize it to achieve organizational goals. A learning culture will help promote both individual learning and shared understanding, and will facilitate the organization to deal with continual change.

To achieve true (and valuable) iterative knowledge, double loop learning encompasses both experimentation and feedback. If the learning organization's culture is strong, new behaviors can be instilled which embrace learning. Argyris (1991) provides an excellent analogy to distinguish between single and double loop learning:

> To give a simple analogy: a thermostat that automatically turns on the heat whenever the temperature in the room drops below 68 degrees is a good example of single-loop learning. A thermostat that could ask "Why am I set at 68 degrees?" and then explore whether or

not some other temperature might more economically achieve the goal of heating the room would be engaging in double-loop learning.

Argyris (1991: 100)

The following schematic (Figure 5.9) depicts the concept of single, double (and even triple) loop learning.

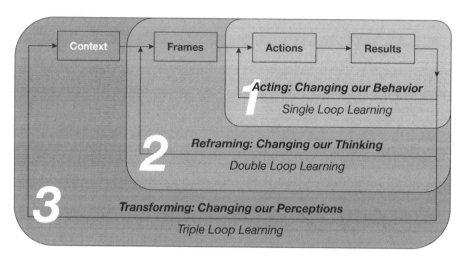

Figure 5.9 *Single, Double and Triple Loop Learning.*

Reproduced with kind permission of Doctrina Applied Research and Consulting LLC—www.consultdoctrina.com

CONCLUSIONS

This chapter has concentrated on the organizational issues of KM. The importance of the organization and its culture have been described in detail as successful organization-wide KM implementation depends on the correct culture being in place. The concept of the learning organization (LO) is of paramount importance to those organizations claiming to be knowledge-empowered.

SUMMARY

This chapter introduced the concept of the learning organization and the importance of this concept to contemporary KM. The importance of organizational culture and how this relates to both the learning organization and contemporary KM was described. The socio-technical issues around KM were also introduced.

REVIEW QUESTIONS

1 What is a learning organization?

2 Describe Senge's five disciplines.

3 What is organizational culture?

4 What is double loop learning?

DISCUSSION QUESTIONS

1 Why is an organization's culture so important when incorporating KM?

2 Why can it be so hard to achieve an effective organizational culture?

CASE EXERCISE: BOEING COMMERCIAL AIRPLANE GROUP[5]

With increased global competition, the Internet, and the rapid rate of development for new technologies, KM is becoming more and more important to organizations in competing in the new global economy. The Boeing Commercial Airplane Group, a division of the Boeing Company, is one of these organizations to utilize KM to gain a sustainable competitive advantage over its rivals. This case exercise will examine Boeing's current use of KM strategies, tools, processes and techniques.

Boeing Overview

The Boeing Company is the world's leading aerospace company. They have a long tradition of technical excellence and innovation. They are the largest manufacturer of commercial jetliners. Boeing is committed to continuously expanding their product line and developing new technologies to meet their customer's needs. Boeing has been the world leader in commercial jetliners for more than forty years and their planes comprise about 75 percent of the world's fleet (Boeing in Brief).

Role of KM at Boeing

The role of KM is very large at Boeing. Boeing currently employs KM to many aspects of the organization. They use KM to gain a competitive edge in the rapidly changing airplane industry. They utilize KM for efficiency, product design innovation, process innovation, error and safety management, and airplane maintenance. The use of KM allows Boeing to tap critical resources of its employees and they apply it to many design and management processes.

103

KM System, Structure and Approach

Boeing's KM system consists of several independent systems and processes. Boeing also has a sharing culture and their approach to KM is top-down and unstructured. Boeing's approach to KM is similar to DuPont in that they both have unstructured approaches and both have a sharing culture. Both of these companies also have many small independent KM systems, instead of one central system. The difference between these two companies is that DuPont has a bottom-up structure, and Boeing has a top-down structure. Management at Boeing realizes the importance and supports all KM efforts. According to Boeing's website: "In today's knowledge economy, knowledge is an organization's most valuable asset and is the only asset that grows in value through reuse" (Knowledge).

Advanced Information Systems Group

Boeing's Advanced Information Systems (AIS) Group is the department that develops all of Boeing's information systems. This also includes Boeing's KM systems. AIS employees consist of Certified Knowledge Managers, Engineers and IT specialists. Their purpose is to create business solutions and add value to the company through IT and best practices (Knowledge).

Boeing Technical Library System

One of Boeing's KM efforts is the Boeing Technical Library System. This is an electronic library that contains a series of topical databases. Topics of the databases consist of: Acronyms, Definitions and Terminology Index, ATA 100 Specifications, Audio/Video, Diagrams and Illustration Inserts Index, Fuel Systems, Hydraulic Power, Illustrated Parts Catalogue, Maintenance Standards, Navigation Systems and Components, and Servicing Procedures. The databases are standardized in presentation, style, format and layout. They also contain internal and external cross-references to eliminate redundancies. The system also includes Executive/Library Directory of Topics and Chapter Titles, Standard Keyword Cross-references for each Topic, and Permuted Keyword Cross-references for the entire Library. All documentation is available through both the Internet and intranets (Boeing 737/200).

Portable Maintenance Aid

Another KM effort at Boeing is their Portable Maintenance Aid (PMA). This is a software tool that is used to support maintenance and engineering activity and helps mechanics troubleshoot jetliners quickly. The software is a digitized library of key technical information stored on CD. The discs can be loaded into a mechanic's laptop for quick access when servicing an airplane. This eliminates the need to repeatedly refer to various manuals and saves time. The software's advanced search capability and hyperlinks connect related references in text, allowing instant access to the Fault Isolation Manual, Aircraft Maintenance Manual, Aircraft Illustrated Parts Catalog, and many other documents. PMA also uses Intelligent graphics technology, which allows users to click on a highlighted area of an illustration and instantly bring up troubleshooting text. PMA software is also network compatible, allowing access by multiple users on a local server (Virgin Atlantic).

Boeing Safety Management System

Boeing also incorporates KM into their Boeing Safety Management System (BSMS). This is a KM process that Boeing uses for flight safety and error management. It is comprised of several tools and aids (Exhibit 1). Boeing conducted a ten-year study which showed that maintenance crew errors and flight crew deviation from established procedures contributed to nearly 20 and 50 percent of all hull-loss accidents. After this study, BSMS was developed to identify the key factors that contributed to crew errors and procedural non-compliance in past accidents.

The BSMS tools are structured analytic processes that operators can use to investigate incidents and develop measures to prevent similar events in the future (see Exhibit 2). BSMS is also used to improve the way incidents are investigated. It focuses on why the event occurs, not who was responsible. BSMS tools also contain a large number of analysis elements that enable the investigator to conduct an in-depth investigation, analyze it, develop recommendations, summarize the findings, enter it into a database, and integrate them across other incidents. It also enables operators to track their progress in addressing the issues revealed by the analyses (BSMS).

The 777 Program

Boeing also incorporates KM into its product design process. The 777 program was a new paperless approach to aircraft development. This project used CAD/CAM (computer-aided design/computer-aided manufacturing) technology and the CATIA (computer-aided three-dimensional interactive application) system to design the 777 airplane. The CAD and CATIA systems allowed design engineers the ability to efficiently design the 777 through the use of three-dimensional models. These three-dimensional models allow designers to view the models from both the interior and exterior of the plane and helped identify any physical interference among various parts and systems and in the 777.

The new technology allowed Boeing engineers to simulate the geometry of an airplane design on the computer without the costly and time-consuming investment of using physical mock-ups. The 777 program also used cross-functional design/build teams. These teams had the task of developing each element of the airplane's airframe or system. In the design/build teams approach, the different specialties involved in airplane development worked jointly to create the airplane's parts and systems. These teams consisted of designers, manufacturing representatives, tooling, engineers, finance and suppliers.

The team members worked concurrently, sharing their knowledge rather than applying their skills sequentially. The 777 program also incorporated customer input into the design process. Communication among the design/build teams was done through the Internet. The findings and lessons learnt from this project were documented for future projects (Computing).

Types of Knowledge at Boeing

The type of knowledge that is collected and used in Boeing's various KM systems, programs and processes were both tacit and explicit. The Technical Library System and PMA consist of explicit

105

knowledge only. They are made up of information that is gathered from various internal and external sources and put into a context. The BSMS process consists of both tacit and explicit knowledge. This is because it uses explicit knowledge from accident publications, findings from studies, and past incident information to analyze and improve safety measures. It also contains tacit knowledge from investigators, experiences of the employees, investigation philosophies, recommendations and lessons learnt. This system collects, analyzes, stores and shares knowledge. The 777 Program also deals

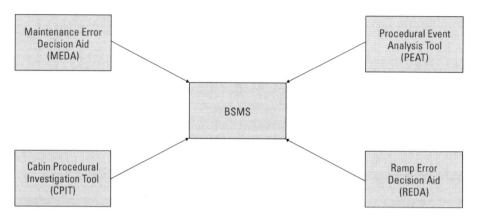

Exhibit 1 *BSMS Structure.*

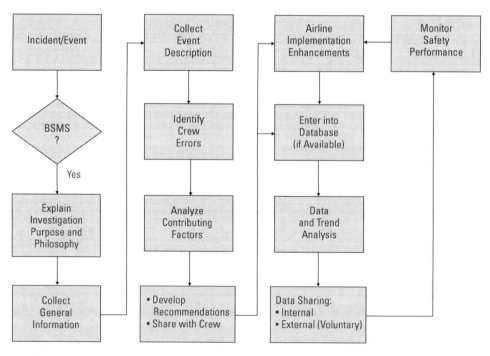

Exhibit 2 *The BSMS Process.*

with tacit and explicit knowledge. Explicit knowledge about the designs and problems of earlier planes was used in this project along with the tacit knowledge of the members of the design/build teams.

A Balanced View of KM at Boeing

A balanced view of KM at Boeing would be that these systems, tools, projects and processes are suitable and effective for Boeing. The KM efforts provide Boeing with many benefits in terms of time and cost savings. Boeing estimates that the PMA reduces the time it takes to search and retrieve information by as much as 40 percent. The 777 Program reduced change and error rework by over 50 percent. KM has also helped streamlined processes and fostered design innovation. On the other hand, these programs and systems are costly and the initial capital investment for these new technologies is very high.

Appropriateness of KM at Boeing

KM is important to Boeing. Their KM approach seems to fit with Boeing's business because they focus on efficiency and innovation. The KM efforts suit the needs of Boeing because it provides them with the knowledge needed to add value to their organization. The knowledge gained from the 777 Program helped Boeing efficiently design a better aircraft. The lessons learnt from this program can also be applied to future design programs. KM at Boeing also helps develop best practices, reduce error and increase efficiency. This is especially true with the BSMS system. This system has allowed Boeing to learn from previous errors and apply these lessons learnt to the prevention of future incidents. The Technical Libraries and PMA allow employees the convenience of quickly and easily accessible explicit knowledge.

Issues/Recommendations

Improvement in KM can be made in adding tacit knowledge to the Technical Libraries and the PMA system. This would be especially helpful in the PMA system. Since the PMA system is used for troubleshooting, having the tacit knowledge such as lessons learnt for specific problems could be helpful in finding solutions. Another issue would be the lack of connection between the various independent KM systems. A recommendation would be for Boeing to integrate these systems.

Another area for improvement would be in the 777 Program. Boeing could develop a formal system to use for future projects that include the experience and lessons learnt from the members of the design/build teams. Boeing could also incorporate message boards and chat rooms for members to collaborate on future projects. Another issue to address would be the increasing complexity of the systems. Boeing does not plan for this. Instead, they either build new systems or expand current ones as the need arises. Another issue to address would be ensuring the reuse of the knowledge captured in the KM systems, where else should they apply KM, and how to maximize the benefits. Recommendations for Boeing are that they should continue to invest in KM and utilize the knowledge resources of their employees for future projects.

Case Exercise References

Boeing Company, *The New York Times*, July 11, 2008.

James Wallace on Aerospace. Available at http://blog.seattlepi.nwsource.com/aerospace/.

The Boeing Company — Hoovers. Available at www.hoovers.com/boeing/.

The Boeing Company. Available at www.boeing.com/.

Vinson, J. (2007) Boeing on Knowledge Management. Available at http://blog.jackvinson.com/archives/2007/10/29/boeing_on_knowledge_management.html.

Case Exercise Questions

1 What are the key issues regarding KM in this case exercise?

2 Is Boeing a knowledge-enabled organization? If so, give some examples of why this is so. If not, what is missing?

3 Given the immense competition in the (global) airline industry, what do you suggest Boeing could do to strategically prepare for the medium to long term?

4 What are the major lessons learnt from this case exercise?

FURTHER READING

Brown, A. (1995) *Organizational Culture*. London: Pitman Publishing.

Davenport, T.H. and Prusak, L. (1998) *Working Knowledge. How Organizations Manage What They Know.* Boston, MA: Harvard Business School Press.

REFERENCES

Alavi, M. and Leidner, D.E. (2001). Knowledge Management and Knowledge Management Systems: Conceptual Foundations and Research Issues, *MIS Quarterly*, 25(1): 107–136.

Anon (1997) Managing Culture. Available online at www.davjac.co.uk (accessed February 19, 1999).

Anthony, R. (1965) *Planning and Control Systems: A Framework for Analysis*. Cambridge, MA: Harvard University Press.

Argyris, C. (1991) Teaching Smart People How to Learn, *Harvard Business Review*, May–June: 99–109.

Argyris, C. and Schön, D. (1978) *Organizational Learning: A Theory of Action Perspective*. Reading, MA: Addison Wesley.

Bali, R.K. (1999) Successful Technology Management: Cultural and Organizational Dimensions of MIS Implementation in SMEs, unpublished Ph.D. thesis, Sheffield Hallam University, U.K.

Bessant, J. and Cole, S. (1985) *Stacking the Chips: Information Technology and the Distribution of Income*. London: Frances Pinter.

Boddy, D. and Gunson, N. (1996) *Organizations in the Network Age*. London: Routledge.

Borman, W.C. (1983) Implications of Personality Theory and Research for the Rating of Work Performance in Organizations, in F.J. Landy, S. Zedeck, and J.N. Cleveland (Eds), *Performance Measurement and Theory*. Hillsdale, NJ: Lawrence Erlbaum Associates, pp. 127–172.

Bower, M. (1966) *The Will to Manage*. New York: McGraw-Hill.

Brown, A. (1995) *Organizational Culture*. London: Pitman Publishing.

Carnall, C. (1995) *Managing Change in Organizations*. Hemel Hempstead: Prentice-Hall.

Coakes, E. (2002) Knowledge Management: A Sociotechnical Perspective, in E. Coakes, D. Willis, and S. Clarke (Eds), *Knowledge Management in the Sociotechnical World*. London: Springer-Verlag, pp. 4–14.

Davenport, T.H. and Prusak, L. (1998) *Working Knowledge. How Organizations Manage What They Know*. Boston, MA: Harvard Business School Press.

David Skyrme Associates (2008) Insights No. 3: The Learning Organization. Available online at www.skyrme. com/insights/3lrnorg.htm (accessed May 19, 2008).

Dudley, J. (1990) *1992: Strategies for the Single Market*. London: Kogan Page.

Earl, M. (1989) *Management Strategies for Information Technology*. Hemel Hempstead: Prentice-Hall.

EDP Analyzer (1986) Organizing for the 1990s. *EDP Analyzer*, 24(1).

Fiedler, K., Grover, V., and Teng, J.T.C. (1994) Information Technology-Enabled Change: The Risks and Rewards of Business Process Redesign and Automation, *Journal of Information Technology*, 9: 267–275.

Flood, R. and Romm, N. (1996) *Diversity Management: Triple Loop Learning*. Chichester: Wiley.

Garrity, J. and Barnes, V. (1968) The Payout in Computers: What Management has Learned about Planning and Control, in W.F. Boore and J.R. Murphy (Eds), *The Computer Sampler: Management Perspectives on the Computer*. New York: McGraw-Hill, Chapter 4.

Gibson, J., Ivancevich, J.M., and Donnelly Jr, J.H. (1994) *Organizations: Behavior, Structure, Processes*. Homewood, IL: Richard D. Irwin.

Gray, P.H. and Meister, D.B. (2003) Introduction: Fragmentation and Integration in Knowledge Management Research, *Information, Technology & People*, 16(3): 259–265.

Gummesson, E. (1988) *Qualitative Methods in Management Research*. Sweden: Chartwell-Bratt.

Gupta, J.D. and Sharma, S.K. (2004) *Creating Knowledge Based Organizations*. Hershey, PA: Idea Group Publishing.

Hampden-Turner, C. (1990) *Creating Corporate Culture*. Reading, MA: Addison-Wesley.

Handy, C. (1985) *Understanding Organizations*, London: Penguin Business.

Harrison, R. (1972) Understanding Your Organization's Character, *Harvard Business Review*, May–June: 119–128.

Hofstede, G. (1993) Cultural Constraints in Management Theories, *Academy of Management Executive*, 7(1): 81–94.

Hofstede, G. (1994) *Cultures and Organizations: Software of the Mind, Intercultural Cooperation and its Importance for Survival*. London: HarperCollins.

Huczynski, A. and Buchanan, D. (1991) *Organizational Behavior*. London: Prentice-Hall.

Hutchison, C. and Rosenberg, D. (1994) The Organization of Organizations: Issues for Next Generation Office IT, *Journal of Information Technology*, 9: 99–117.

Jackson, T. (1995) *Virgin King*. London: HarperCollins.

Johnson, G. (1992) Managing Strategic Change—Strategy, Culture and Action, *Long Range Planning*, 25(1): 28–36.

Johnston, H. and Vitale, M. (1988) Creating Competitive Advantage with Interorganisational Information Systems, *MIS Quarterly*, June: 153–165.

Kroeber, A. and Kluckhohn, C. (1952) *Culture: A Critical Review of Concepts and Definitions.* Cambridge, MA: Vintage Books.

Laver, M. (1989) *Information Technology: Agent of Change.* Cambridge: Cambridge University Press.

Licker, P. (1997) *Management Information Systems: A Strategic Leadership Approach.* Orlando, FL: The Dryden Press.

Long, L. (1989) *Management Information Systems.* Upper Saddle River, NJ: Prentice-Hall.

Lucas, H. (1990) *Information Systems Concepts for Management.* Singapore: McGraw-Hill.

Lucey, T. (1991) *Management Information Systems.* Guernsey: Guernsey Press.

March, J. and Simon, H. (1958) *Organizations.* New York: Wiley.

Mintzberg, H. (1989) *Mintzberg on Management: Inside Our World of Organizations.* New York: Free Press.

Nonaka, I. and Takeuchi, H. (1995) *The Knowledge-Creating Company.* New York: Oxford University Press.

Pedler, M., Burgoyne, J., and Boydell, T. (1991) *The Learning Company. A Strategy for Sustainable Development.* London: McGraw-Hill.

Pennings, J. (1993) Executive Reward Systems: A Cross-Cultural Comparison, *Journal of Management Studies,* 30(2): 261–280.

Pheysey, D. (1993) *Organizational Cultures: Types and Transformations.* London: Routledge.

Polanyi, M. (1967) *The Tacit Dimension.* New York: Anchor Books.

Porter, M. (1985) *Competitive Advantage: Creating and Sustaining Superior Performance.* New York: Free Press.

Reference for Business (2008) Management Information Systems (MIS). Available online at www.reference forbusiness.com/small/Mail-Op/Management-Information-Systems-MIS.html (accessed May 24, 2008).

Robbins, S. (1991) *Management.* Upper Saddle River, NJ: Prentice-Hall.

Schein, E. (1990) Organizational Culture, *American Psychologist,* 45(2): 109–119.

Schultheis, R. and Sumner, M. (1995) *Management Information Systems: The Manager's View.* New York: Richard D. Irwin.

Scott-Morton, M. (1995) Emerging Organizational Forms: Work and Organization in the 21st Century, *European Management Journal,* 13(4): 339–345.

Senge, P.M. (1992) *The Fifth Discipline — The Art & Practice of the Learning Organization.* London: Century Business.

Smircich, L. (1983) Concepts of Culture and Organizational Analysis, *Administrative Science Quarterly,* 28: 339–358.

Spender, J.C. (1994) Method, Philosophy and Empirics in KM and IC, *Journal of Intellectual Capital,* 7(1): 12–28.

Thornhill, A. (1993) Management Training Across Cultures: The Challenge for Trainers, *Journal of European Industrial Training,* 17(10): 43–51.

Tylor, E. (1871, 1903) *Primitive Culture: Researches into the Development of Mythology, Philosophy, Religion, Language, Art and Custom.* Murray: London.

Vitell, S.J., Nwachukwu, J.L., and Barnes, J.H. (1993) The Effects of Culture on Ethical Decision-Making: An Application of Hofstede's Typology, *Journal of Business Ethics,* 12: 753–760.

Ward, J. and Peppard, J. (1995) *Reconciling the IT/Business Relationship: A Troubled Marriage in Need of Guidance,* Working Paper Series, Cranfield School of Management, SWP2/95. Cranfield: Cranfield University.

Williams, A., Dobson, P., and Walters, M. (1993) *Changing Culture: New Organizational Approaches.* London: Institute of Personnel Management.

Wiseman, C. (1985) *Strategy and Computers.* New York: Free Press.

Zmud, R. (1984) Design Alternatives for Organizing Information Systems Activities, *MIS Quarterly,* June: 79–93.

Chapter 6

Applying Knowledge

INTRODUCTION

As has been discussed in previous chapters, KM is essential for organizations to attain and/or maintain a sustainable competitive advantage. What becomes of significance then, is how to apply the knowledge that has been created and stored within the organization. If the application of knowledge doesn't lead to value or benefit for the organization, the measures taken to capture, store and disseminate the knowledge to those who should use it becomes a largely futile exercise.

This chapter then serves to explore the two areas of creating value from KM, applications of KM, as well as succeeding with KM and its relevance to industry. In so doing, two respective approaches: the OODA Loop by Boyd (Wickramasinghe and von Lubitz, 2007) and the intelligence continuum by Wickramasinghe and Schaffer (2006) are described.

CREATING VALUE FROM KNOWLEDGE

A critical function for organizations and, more specifically, managers is decision making. Unstructured decision making requires the gathering of multi-spectral data and information if the decision maker is to make a prudent choice (Wickramasinghe and von Lubitz, 2007). Unstructured decision making in dynamic and complex environments is always challenging and the decision maker is always at a point of information inferiority (von Lubitz and Wickramasinghe, 2006c). It is in such situations that the need for germane knowledge, pertinent information and relevant data are critical (ibid.) and hence the value of knowledge to an organization is best evidenced.

Hierarchically, the gathering of information precedes the transformation of information into useable knowledge (Alavi and Leidner, 1999; Massey, 2002). Hence, the rate of information collection and the quality of the collected information will have a major impact on the quality (usefulness) of the generated knowledge (Award and Ghaziri, 2004).

During the past twenty years the world of business has changed, and its prior West-dominated stability has transformed into the present volatile environment of political, economical and social tensions (Drucker, 1999; Courtney, 2001; Shin, 2004). While the laws of supply and demand are still the foundation of the global economy, the concept of competitiveness left the traditional boundaries of "better, cheaper, faster," and must now also include the profound sense of global awareness and sensitivity to factors that were once considered as minor or even inconsequential.

This new environment of global business generates and, in order to be successful, requires vast quantities of multi-spectral data from sources as divergent (and seemingly irrelevant) as geography and the nature of local religions (Drucker, 1999; Courtney, 2001; Shin, 2004). In order to be meaningful, the widely dispersed and apparently disconnected (or irrelevant) data must be processed into coherent information. The latter must then be rapidly converted into a knowledge-base that, in turn, serves as the foundation for the purposeful and flexible rule-set that allows goal-oriented interactions with the environment within which business transactions are conducted (Drucker, 1999; Brown and Duguid, 2002).

In the dynamic and, to a large degree, unpredictable world of global business, "action space awareness" (or synonymous "competitive space awareness") and information superiority (Boyd, 1976; von Lubitz and Wickramasinghe, 2006a) have become the key factors to all successful operations. Such awareness, however, can only be enabled through the extraction of multi-spectral data.

Boyd's OODA Loop (Figure 6.1) provides a formalized analysis of the processes involved in the development of a superior strategy (Boyd, 1987; Cebrowski and Garstka, 1998; Alberts *et al.*, 2000; von Lubitz and Wickramasinghe, 2006a,b) and a suitable model to facilitate the organizing of germane knowledge.

The Loop is based on a cycle of four interrelated stages revolving in time and space: Observation followed by Orientation, then by Decision, and finally Action. At the Observation and Orientation stages, multi-spectral implicit and explicit inputs are gathered (Observation) and converted into coherent information (Orientation). The latter determines the sequential Determination (knowledge generation) and Action (practical implementation of knowledge) steps.

The outcome of the latter affects, in turn, the character of the starting point (Observation) of the next revolution in the forward progression of the rolling loop. The Orientation stage specifies the characteristics and the nature of the "center of thrust" at which the effort is to concentrate during the Determination and Action stages.

Hence, the Loop implicitly incorporates the rule of "economy of force," i.e. the requirement that only minimum but adequate (containment) effort is applied to insignificant aspects of competitive interaction. The Loop exists as a network of simultaneous and intertwined events that characterize the multidimensional action space (competition space), and both influence and are influenced by the actor (e.g. an organization) at the center of the network. Moreover, the events provide the context and search criteria for extracting germane knowledge.

SUCCEEDING WITH KM

Not only is it important to at all times ensure that germane knowledge is being extracted, it is also essential that KM does indeed provide a sustained advantage. This necessitates a long term rather than single focus, which in turn requires the continual analysis of the current

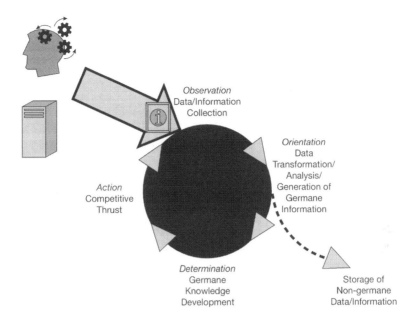

Figure 6.1 *Boyd's OODA Loop.*

Reproduced with kind permission of Doctrina Applied Research and Consulting LLC—www.consultdoctrina.com

situation and extant knowledge base and then building upon this so that at all times the future state benefits from the lessons gained in the current state. To aid in this regard Wickramasinghe and Schaffer (2006) developed the intelligence continuum.

The intelligence continuum consists of a collection of key tools, techniques and processes of the knowledge economy; i.e. including data mining, business intelligence/analytics and KM, which are applied to a generic system of people, process and technology in a systematic and ordered fashion (Wickramasinghe and Schaffer, 2006). Taken together they represent a very powerful instrument for refining the data raw material stored in data marts and/or data warehouses and thereby maximizing the value and utility of these data assets. As depicted in Figure 6.2, the intelligence continuum is applied to the output of the generic information system.

Once applied, the results become part of the data set that are reintroduced into the system and combined with the other inputs of people, processes and technology to develop an improvement continuum. Thus, the intelligence continuum includes the generation of data, the analysis of these data to provide a "diagnosis" and the reintroduction into the cycle as a "prescriptive" solution.

The key capabilities and power of the model are in analyzing large volumes of disparate, multi-spectral data so that superior decision making can ensue. This is achieved through the incorporation of the various intelligence tools and techniques, which taken together make it possible to analyze all data elements in aggregate. Currently, most analysis of data is applied to single data sets and uses at most two of these techniques (Nonaka, 1994; Nonaka and Nishiguchi, 2001; Newell *et al.*, 2002; Schultze and Leidner, 2002; Wickramasinghe, 2006;

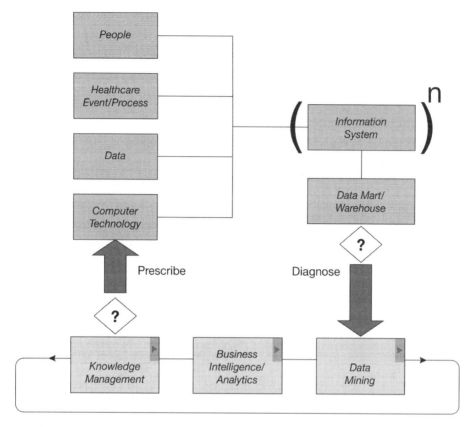

Figure 6.2 *The Intelligence Continuum.*

Source: adapted from Wickramasinghe and Schaffer (2006)

Wickramasinghe and Schaffer, 2006). Thus, there is neither the power nor the capabilities to analyze large volumes of multi-spectral data (Nonaka, 1994).

Moreover, the interaction with domain experts is typically non-existent in current methods. Applying these capabilities then to any complex scenario, the benefits of the intelligence continuum model are profound indeed, since the tools and techniques of the intelligence continuum can serve to transform the situation of information inferiority to one of information superiority in real time through the effective and efficient processing of disparate, diverse and seemingly unrelated data. This will then enable decision makers to make superior decisions and chaos will be lessened and order restored.

APPLICATIONS OF KM

KM is universally applicable and of universal benefit to most situations. Currently there are few areas that cannot benefit from the application of KM tools and techniques. To emphasize this important point, three different scenarios are presented. The first scenario is concerned with the consulting industry, the second focuses on emergency and disaster instances, while the third

Table 6.1 *Applications of KM*

Scenario	Benefit from KM
Consulting companies	Many of the consulting companies were facing several challenges including trying to retain key employees, not being able to meet clients expectations and facing mergers and acquisitions.
	KM is embraced to capture employees' tacit knowledge and important lessons, develop knowledge bases to store key explicit knowledge and facilitate knowledge sharing between employees as well as between employees and clients.
Emergency and Disaster Scenarios (E&DS)	Irrespective of location and/or country and irrespective of whether the disaster is man made or natural in all E&DS the situation is dynamic and complex and rapid action is required. Further, information inferiority is a huge problem to decision makers.
	KM (examples include OODA Loop and Intelligence Continuum as well as products being developed currently by Microsoft) is useful to facilitate the decision maker to make superior decisions as well as to help training via simulation a priori.
Orthopedic surgery	In knee replacements, which are becoming more prevalent due to the large percentage of aging populations, many factors must be considered if the outcome is to be a success.
	KM both tacit knowledge and explicit knowledge is key in facilitating the surgeon's decision making processes be it choice of implant, medications for preventing infection and facilitating recovery to even the appropriate physiotherapy regimen.

provide the example of orthopedic surgery and decisions pertaining to knee reconstruction. Table 6.1 serves to summarize why and how KM is beneficial in all these contexts.

We now describe each of these three examples in greater detail.

Scenario 1: Consulting Companies

The management consulting industry is far from homogenous and it can be thought of as having several different segments of players. Three major segments are as follows:

- Generalist/Strategy;
- The Big CPA Firms; and
- IT focused companies.[6]

Contemporaneously with changing client needs and expectations, many of these companies were experiencing mergers and globalization pressures. The combination of these distinct, yet not necessarily unrelated needs, was that these firms had to adapt. Specifically, strategies were required to address these new business needs and systems were needed to support the new business processes. KM was identified to be the strategy to adopt in order to provide these firms with a new vision for managing their internal knowledge resources. KM systems were

115

identified as the systems to implement in order to support and enable the required business processes that would ensure the realization of this new strategic direction.

The investments by these firms in KM have been significant indeed. Some initial costs were as much as 12 million with about 10 percent of revenues annually required for building and managing the knowledge capital. Such investments demonstrate a belief on the part of these firms that KM is key to enable these organizations to maintain their competitive advantage. It can be seen that the need for—and application of—KM for all the consulting companies has been critical for providing better solutions to their clients, having better and faster access to data and information that is dispersed through many offices and residing in various databases, and also capturing important lessons to be re-used in future client engagements.

Scenario 2: Emergency and Disaster Scenarios (E&DS)

The need for more effective, superior crisis management techniques is clearly becoming apparent as we embark upon post crisis analysis for each of the more recent disasters from 9/11, to the Tsunami in December 2004, the floods in Europe, hurricanes Katrina and Rita, the earthquakes in Pakistan and terrible floods in China in 2008. This area is the focus for the emerging discipline of Operations Other than War (OOTW). Commonly considered as military, OOTW now becomes increasingly civilian-driven, and often executed as interventions in potentially unstable environments, or as management activities consequent to destabilizing events.

In addition to the most obvious topic of terrorism, where risk assessment and management are prerogative to meaningful counteraction, problems of assessing and managing consequences of natural disasters, epidemic diseases, major industrial or transportation accidents, or humanitarian relief operations, become increasingly relevant. What do these situations all have in common apart from causing massive disruption and tremendous loss of life; they are all extremely dynamic and complex scenarios where decision makers must make critical decisions with far reaching consequences from a position of extreme information inferiority.

Once again, such situations are most suitable for the application of KM; in particular, both OODA Loop thinking so that germane knowledge and pertinent information can be extracted and passed onto the decision maker but also the application of the intelligence continuum so that it is possible to analyze past incidents and prepare more refined rubrics for how to deploy relief and aid more efficiently and effectively. It is interesting to note that Microsoft is currently developing disaster management software that draws heavily on the tools, techniques, tactics and technologies of KM to provide simulations and thereby aid decision makers in such emergency and disaster situations, both in terms of enhancing training a priori as well as facilitation in situ decision making.[7]

Scenario 3: Orthopedic Surgery

Advancing age often leads to the degeneration of the knee and hip joints, so that reconstruction of the joint is often required. Given the increasing number of the population who will be over the age of sixty-five over the next forty years, in countries facing the inverted population pyramid, these devices are being implanted in increasingly larger numbers during major surgical procedures, in which the degenerative joint surfaces are removed and replaced with artificial components.

There are a multitude of variables in these reconstructions, ranging from the patient's characteristics and healthcare status to the implant design and implantation methodologies. The surgeon's tacit knowledge determines the "best" implant design and combinations and implantation methodologies that are used for each particular patient. The examination of the clinical results leads to the explicit knowledge that determines if those choices are appropriate for each patient population.

It is also possible to analyze such a dynamic scenario in terms of the intelligence continuum; this time the antecedent events would be the previous experience of the surgeon, the source events would be the current data, the transformations would be the transformations effected by the knowledge spiral and enabled through data mining techniques, and the consequences would be the better treatment outcomes for patients.

RELEVANCE TO INDUSTRY

In some sections of the industrial sector, there remains much debate as to the true value of KM in the contemporary workplace. Whether this is due to unfulfilled promises of the potential of previous ICT-driven initiatives or the belief that KM offers a "silver bullet" solution is a matter of opinion. As we have discussed in this Primer, the value of KM depends on correct implementation which, in turn, depends on both technical and non-technical considerations. By way of example, several companies operating in the legal sector have embraced KM as their KMS enables them to communicate and disseminate legal knowledge via (internal or external) wikis, allows them to use their Personal Digital Assistants (PDAs) to remain in close contact with their offices/clients from the courtroom and paves the way towards "e-filing"—a KM-enabled solution whereby litigation and court-based documents can be sent securely and quickly using the existing internet infrastructure.

It is entirely possible that existing back-office systems would need to be quickly upgraded to catch up with such innovations—making a mockery of the argument that KM is merely IT-driven. KM has also integrated with marketing functions and operations. The effective use of extranets has allowed companies to store information for clients (again either internal or external).

With information overload affecting most workers, companies that rely heavily (or, indeed, entirely) on the internet for their daily operations (such as Amazon.com) are testament to the value of KM tools and techniques. The use of innovative filtering and AI (Artificial Intelligence)-based calculations allow the Amazon website to seamlessly proffer to the user "suggested" book, CD and DVD titles. This "may be relevant for you" approach has a "domino effect"—each offered suggestion has attached and associated additional suggestions. The filtering system identifies patterns of common interest—this allows the system to collect several users' preferences and offer "Customers who bought this item also bought" suggestions. The link to CoPs (or communities of interest) and social networks is clear. A wide range of international organizations have had great success with various KM initiatives. These include (Sveiby, 2006) such companies as:

General Electric's Answer Center (U.S.)

Since 1982, GE has collected customer complaints in a database that supports telephone operators in answering customer calls. The company has input 1.5 million potential problems and their solutions into its system.

Frito-Lay (U.S.)

Data on shelf space utilization is collected on a daily basis by sales representatives for all brands. This data is combined with market information and fed back to the representatives who pass this (best shelf utilization) on to the retailers.

Dow Chemical (U.S.)

The company has put 25,000 patents into a central database that is accessible by all Dow divisions who can explore how existing patents can gain more revenues. This approach is now being applied to intellectual assets (e.g. branding).

British Petroleum

KM is used as means of bringing together talents from all over the organization. The company emphasizes transfer of tacit knowledge, which is carried out via their communications network comprising video-conferencing, multi-media and email.

Xerox (U.S.)

The company has provided convenient places where people can routinely get together. They refer to these environments as "distributed coffee pots" in order to encourage cross-functional links.

SUMMARY AND CONCLUSIONS

In order to successfully incorporate KM, an organization must give careful consideration to how extract germane knowledge pertinent information and relevant data if it is to truly derive the full value from KM. In this chapter, one systematic yet elegant method for ensuring that at all times germane knowledge is provided to the decision maker is via Boyd's OODA Loop and the consequent application of OODA thinking. In addition, the chapter presented a systematic and robust method for ensuring that an organization continues to succeed with KM; namely the intelligence continuum which is always focused on enhancing the current state and existing knowledge base. Finally, the chapter provided scenarios of applications of KM to underscore the universality of KM to all organizations, as well as presented a discussion on how it is relevant to industry.

REVIEW QUESTIONS

1 Describe the four stages of Boyd's OODA Loop.

2 Why is it essential to have germane knowledge?

3 Why do we say the business environment is dynamic and complex?

4 Why has intelligence gathering become so important?

5 Describe how the Intelligence Continuum enhances the extant knowledge base?

6 Describe scenarios where KM is useful?

DISCUSSION QUESTIONS

1 Why does the OODA Loop always enable an organization to have germane knowledge and stay ahead of its competition?

2 Can you think of a situation where KM would not be helpful and why?

CASE EXERCISE: THE NEED FOR KM AT NORTHROP GRUMMAN[8]

Introduction

In the late 1990s Northrop Grumman (NG) senior level management were contemplating the challenge of "how to successfully downsize and yet retain the knowledge and expertise residing in employees' heads." The dilemma of needing to downsize and yet retain as much know-how as possible is not uncommon for many companies, especially government agencies. In fact, by 2010 more than half the U.S. work force will be over forty, so addressing the matter of keeping critical technical expertise and know-how will become more and more important.

NG turned to KM as an appropriate solution and nearly ten years later the company uses a variety of tools to retain and transfer vital knowledge in the form of expertise and know-how. Based on the experience of NG it would appear that KM holds the key to preventing a massive brain drain in the future.

Background

Northrop Grumman (NG) is an aerospace and defense company that resulted from the purchase of Grumman by Northrop in 1994. Today, employing over 122,000 people and with annual revenues of over $30 billion, the company is the third largest defense contractor for the U.S. military and the number one company building of naval vessels in the U.S.

The company has several autonomous business units, including: Information and Services, Electronics, Aerospace and Ships. NG's Integrated Systems, headquartered in Dallas, Texas is a leading aerospace systems integration enterprise. IT has the capabilities to design, develop, integrate, produce and support complete systems as well as airframe subsystems for airborne surveillance and battle management aircraft, early warning aircraft, airborne electronic warfare aircraft and air combat aircraft. Currently, it is also focusing on integrating these capabilities for emerging network-centric warfare concepts.

In the late 1990s and shortly after the merger, air combat systems (ACS), a business area within the Integrated Systems sector at NG was consolidating and downsizing. Especially with the end of the Cold War it was felt that this was a prudent strategy. However, such a direction brought with it numerous headaches.

ACS was the lead contractor for the B-2 Stealth Bomber, an aircraft that was nearing the end of its production life, and expertise was literally walking out of the door. ACS was in grave danger of losing the knowledge and skills required to support and maintain this complex machine that would indeed be flying, carrying precious cargo and lives for many years to come.

KM at NG

John Smith, the project manager, decided that in order to prevent further loss of knowledge and expertise it would be necessary for ACS to implement an appropriate KM initiative. However, he was convinced that before he could launch a successful KM initiative throughout the El Segundo, California based NG business unit, it was necessary to get a deeper understating of what barriers, if any, prevented employees from sharing knowledge with their peers.

He was convinced that if he could apply hard numbers to ACS's cultural attitudes about knowledge, he'd have a good handle for a unit-wide KM program and this would then enable him to get the funding needed for the technologies required to facilitate the initiative. To do this Smith decided to conduct a knowledge audit that had two main objectives — 1) to assess ACS's readiness for a formal KM effort, 2) to highlight the areas where sharing was not happening.

The audit was conducted by Boston-based Delphi Group. One of the key benefits of this audit was that it enabled Smith to "turn gut feeling into numbers." It also helped Smith to develop an appropriate strategy to pinpoint who in the outfit had the important knowledge they needed to capture.

KM at ACS

In the late 1990s the B-2 bomber program was winding down and engineers with twenty or more years of experience were leaving. At this time ACS decided to establish a ten-person KM team to identify subject matter experts and capture their expertise and knowledge.

To do this, they constructed approximately 100 knowledge categories called cells, including: armaments, software engineering, manufacturing, etc. In addition, they identified 200 subject matter experts within these cells. Contemporaneously, the KM council turned its attention to knowledge capture. The team created websites for each cell and carefully logged information about the knowledge experts into an expert locator system called Xref. Using Xref, employees could search for information in numerous ways such as employee name, program affiliation or skill.

The B-2 KM effort was deemed a success. So much so that in 1999, when ACS announced a reorganization that would cut the workforce from 8,000—6,000, ACS again turned to KM and decided to establish a four-person KM team charged with developing a unit-wide strategy. To do this, John Smith, the project manager, was convinced that the audit was integral to the ultimate success of this project. In particular, Smith wanted to make sure that the information that was captured was not only useful but would be used and re-used.

The Knowledge Audit

The knowledge audit was conducted by administering a survey designed to unearth employee attitudes about knowledge and knowledge sharing, and in so doing identify areas for improvement. For example, a question on the survey was "From your perspective, to what extent is the knowledge that you and your team generate reused by other teams?"

The survey was emailed to over 4,700 employees at ACS in the six locations across the country. In addition, about 200 employees on the shop floor received paper-based surveys. Participation was voluntary and employees received a free lunch. The final response rate was close to 3,400 or about 70 percent.

The surveys were completed in January and February 2000. In March 2000, Delphi consultants analyzed preliminary results and targeted 125 employees for face-to-face follow up interviews.

Results from the Survey

The survey results confirmed John Smith's concern that sharing knowledge across programs was problematic; however John was pleasantly surprised to learn that employees did recognize the value of using and utilizing know-how from their colleagues as well as the general willingness to share information. This was unexpected indeed. Specifically, 75 percent noted that knowledge was either very or somewhat important, while 51 percent recognized the value of tacit knowledge and affirmed that "the brains of ACS employees were the primary source for best practices."

The results from the survey provided the support that a sharing culture existed and that employees valued knowledge, most particularly tacit knowledge. Form this, a three-pronged strategy that focused on people, process and technology was developed.

People

The KM team set out to identify and then retain experts throughout the ACS. One such CoP consisted of ACS project managers. It was true that such communities existed informally, but Smith strongly felt that if these informal groups were not formalized, their strategic importance and visibility would be lost. The critical objective of these CoPs was to foster and nurture sharing of knowledge across boundaries.

Processes

To address process issues, the KM team focused on finding out how people captured, organized and re-used existing knowledge. Currently there was no central repository where lessons learnt could be stored and later accessed, so the team decided to design and implement such a system. For example, the F/A-18 fighter jet program has such a web-based system. In addition, focus was given to integrating KM to the tracking system.

Technology

The KM team recognized the need to integrate various KM systems at ACS. Tools such as the Xref system, document management systems and collaboration applications were designed and developed. Given that the survey results indicated that people would share information if a convenient system was in place, five critical systems were developed including a portal, expert locator, knowledge capture and media management.

Essentially, and by 2004, the technology supporting KM at NG interfaces and complements NEET (Network Enterprise Engineering Toolkit). NEET was designed to assemble established engineering processes, techniques and tools to provide a capability to meet evolving customer telecommunication requirements. The idea was that NEET would facilitate and support the "systematic process of finding, selecting, organizing, distilling and presenting information in a way that improves employees' comprehension of a specific area of interest" (Clemens *et al.*, 2004). It was well understood that what was key was to develop a common framework so that personnel throughout the company could access what was necessary. Figure F depicts the basic approach for NEET while Figure G provides a useful schematic of key elements of the logical design of NEET.

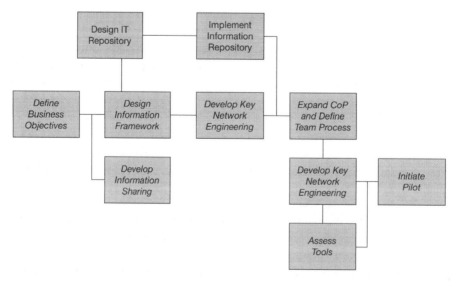

Figure F *The Basic Approach for NEET.*

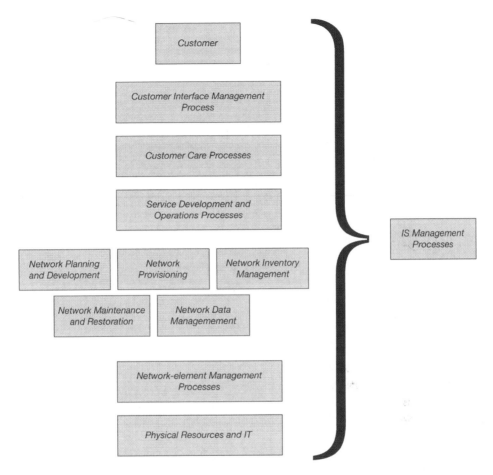

Figure G *A Schematic of Key Elements of the Logical Design of NEET.*

Future

As the number of employees starts to plateau, the goals and objectives of the KM system will gradually change from one of knowledge capture to one of trying to enhance innovation and speed of responsiveness to customers. This will also mean that the ROI will then need to measure whether innovation and speed translate into cost savings for the customer. Smith pondered the future direction for KM at ACS and wondered what he should do next. Since the start of the KM project times had changed for NG.

While a large portion of its workforce was nearing retirement age, the average age of employees had decreased and the company was starting to hire more college graduates. To Smith it seemed that now would be a good time to think about how to balance a more gradual transfer of knowledge from older to younger employees. He had a few ideas but the road ahead was nowhere near clearly shaped as yet. One of the other areas of concern for Smith was to design and develop a system that could measure the ROI of the KM system being developed.

However, he was pleased that KM was now a key business strategy at NG, which had allowed them to identify, capture and transfer knowledge so employees could leverage from this "in-house" expertise to provide better products and services for their customers and he knew that KM would be an integral component no matter what the future directive would be.

Conclusions

The NG case exercise represents a most interesting experience with KM. It is surprising that in a time of downsizing, employees were actually willing to share their knowledge when the end result might mean they would be losing their own job. The concept of the knowledge audit is misleading because knowledge was never audited, rather the survey was used as an instrument to glean beliefs and attitudes towards KM , knowledge a well as various tools and techniques used in KM.

Case Exercise References

www.cio.com/archive/090101/thanks.html?printversion=yes.

www.cio.com/article/print/16548.

http://en.wikipedia.org/wiki/Northrop_Grumman.

www.irconnect.com/noc/pages/news_printer.html?d=26972&print=1.

www.northropgrumman.com/.

Clemens, R., Seelman, P., Knopman, R., and Chong, H. (2004) Use of Knowledge Management Techniques to Improve Network Engineering Capabilities, *Technology Review Journal*, Spring/Summer: 49–69.

Case Exercise Questions

1 Why did the employees agree to participate and share knowledge when the downsize was occurring?

2 What were the critical success components to NG's KM initiative?

3 How successful do you think NG will be in transitioning their KM system from one of storing knowledge to one of facilitating innovation and faster customer response time—why?

4 What are the key lessons from this case exercise?

FURTHER READING

Boyd, J.R. (1976, 2002) Destruction and Creation, in R. Coram (Ed.), *Boyd*. New York: Little, Brown & Co, pp. 451–462.

Davenport, T. and Prusak, L. (1998) *Working Knowledge*. Boston, MA: Harvard Business School Press.

Liebowitz, J. (2008) *Making Cents Out of Knowledge Management*. Lanham, MD: Scarecrow Press.

Wickramasinghe, N. and von Lubitz, D. (2007) *Knowledge-Based Enterprise Theories and Fundamentals*. Hersey, PA: IGI.

Wigg, K. (1993) *Knowledge Management Foundations*. Arlington, VA: Schema Press.

REFERENCES

Alavi, M. and Leidner, D. (1999) Knowledge Management Systems: Issues, Challenges and Benefits, *Communications of the Association for Information Systems*, 1 Paper #5

Alberts, D., Garstka, J., and Stein, F. (2000) Network Centric Warfare: Developing and Leveraging Information Superiority, *CCRP Publication Series* Washington, DC: Dept. of Defense, pp. 1–284. Available at www.dodccrp.org/publications/pdf/Alberts_NCW.pdf.

Award, E. and Ghaziri, H. (2004) *Knowledge Management*. Upper Saddle River, NJ: Prentice-Hall.

Boyd, J. (1976, 2002) Destruction and Creation, in R. Coram (Ed.), *Boyd*. New York: Little, Brown & Co, pp. 451–462.

Boyd, J. (1987) in Patterns of Conflict, unpublished briefing. Available online as Essence of Winning and Losing, at www.d-n-i.net.

Brown, J. and Duguid, P. (2002) *The Social Life of Information*. Boston, MA: Harvard Business School Press.

Cebrowski, A. and Garstka, J. (1998) Network-Centric Warfare: Its Origin and Future, *Proceedings Magazine*, USNI, 1: 28–35.

Courtney, J. (2001) Decision Making and Knowledge Management in Inquiring Organizations: Toward a New Decision-Making Paradigm for DSS, *Decision Support Systems Special Issue on Knowledge Management*, 31: 17–38.

Drucker, P. (1993) *Post-Capitalist Society*. New York: HarperCollins.

Drucker, P. (1999) Beyond the Information Revolution, *The Atlantic Monthly*, October: 47–57.

Massey, A., Montoya-Weiss, M., and O'Driscoll, T. (2002) Knowledge Management in Pursuit of Performance: Insights from Nortel Networks, *MIS Quarterly*, 26(3): 269–289.

Newell, S., Robertson, M., Scarbrough, H., and Swan, J. (2002) *Managing Knowledge Work*. New York: Palgrave.

Nonaka, I. (1994) A Dynamic Theory of Organizational Knowledge Creation, *Organizational Science*, 5: 14–37.

Nonaka, I. and Nishiguchi, T. (2001) *Knowledge Emergence*. Oxford: Oxford University Press.

Schultze, U. and Leidner, D. (2002) Studying Knowledge Management in Information Systems Research: Discourses and Theoretical Assumptions, *MIS Quarterly*, 26(3): 212–242.

Shin, M. (2004) A Framework for Evaluating Economies of Knowledge Management Systems, *Information & Management*, 42(1): 179–196.

Sveiby, J. (2006) Knowledge Management Initiatives Round the Globe. Available online at www.sveiby.com/KnowledgeManagementInitiativesRoundtheGlobe/tabid/123/Default.aspx (accessed July 31, 2008).

von Lubitz, D. and Wickramasinghe, N. (2006a) Healthcare and Technology: The Doctrine of Network-Centric Healthcare, *International Journal of Electronic Healthcare*, 4: 322–344.

von Lubitz, D. and Wickramasinghe, N. (2006b) Dynamic Leadership in Unstable and Unpredictable Environments, *International Journal of Innovation and Learning*, 4: 339–350.

von Lubitz, D. and Wickramasinghe, N. (2006c) Creating Germane Knowledge in Dynamic Environments, *International Journal of Innovation and Learning*, 3(3): 326–347.

Wickramasinghe, N. (2006) Knowledge Creation: A Meta-Framework, *International Journal of Innovation and Learning*, 3(5): 558–573.

Wickramasinghe, N. and von Lubitz, D. (2007) *Knowledge-Based Enterprise Theories and Fundamentals*. Hersey, PA: IGI.

Wickramasinghe, N. and Schaffer, J. (2006) Creating Knowledge Driven Healthcare Processes with the Intelligence Continuum, *International Journal of Electronic Healthcare*, 2(2): 164–174.

Epilogue

The aim of this book was to demystify the usefulness of KM in the workplace. KM is a relatively nascent field of discovery and while there are several books on the market which discuss various aspects, we have met and conversed with many people who feel that KM is just IT in another guise. This has troubled us since KM is much more. We hope that this book has dispelled this myth and shown that, when executed correctly, management of knowledge can have a powerful and long-term effect; in fact KM is possibly the only source of sustainable competitive advantage for any organization.

Throughout this book, we have emphasized the importance of effectively combining *people, process* and *technology*. This concept is, of course, very simple; correct implementation of the concept in organizations is much more difficult. By adopting a "bottom up" approach to the various components and aspects of KM, we have laid down the foundations for understanding this critical area and we hope that we have encouraged readers to delve further into this most exciting domain.

The world of business is dynamic and KM is an evolving field; undoubtedly there will be many exciting innovations as this evolution occurs. In 1597, Sir Francis Bacon wrote that *"Ipsa scientia potestas est"*—translated from the Latin, this means that "knowledge itself is power." If it was true then, it is even more true and valid today—tomorrow, it should be still more important. We hope that this book has demonstrated that organizational knowledge can mean organizational power.

Glossary

Boyd's Loop (or OODA Loop)　A cycle of four interrelated stages revolving in time and space (observation, orientation, decision and action) aimed at trying to ensure action. The last stage is based on germane knowledge and relevance to the given context, thereby ensuring that it is superior to any other action that might have been contemplated.

BPR　Business process re-engineering—the radical redesign of processes in an organization to make them more effective and efficient.

Combination　The transformation of explicit knowledge into new explicit knowledge.

Community of Practice　Networks of people who work on similar processes or in similar disciplines, and who come together to develop and share their knowledge in that field for the benefit of both themselves and their organizations.

Competitive Advantage　The relative (against rivals) beneficial differentiation in the market of an organization, by means of cost, market position, product or service.

Critical Systems Thinking　Critical systems thinking attempts to bring together systems thinking, participatory methods and reflection to help address boundary judgements and complexity, with particular regard to power structures. Compare with Hard Systems Thinking and Soft Systems Thinking.

Data　A series of discrete events, observations, measurements or facts, which can take the form of numbers, words, sounds and/or images.

Data Analysis　Typically used to sort through data in order to identify patterns and establish relationships.

Data Sharing　Sharing and disseminating data with colleagues and collaborators, international entities, or making data available to the wider public.

Data Warehousing　A generic term for a system for storing, retrieving and managing large amounts of any type of data. Data warehouse software often includes sophisticated compression and hashing techniques for fast searches, as well as advanced filtering.

Database	An organized body of related information.
Declarative Knowledge	Knowledge of what exists and what does not — knowing "that." Declarative knowledge is about facts, concepts and inference. Compare with Procedural Knowledge.
Double Loop Learning	The ability to challenge and rethink the assumptions, routines, standards and decisions within an organization.
Emergent Properties	The Emergent Property of a system is the thing that the system is able to do that its component parts cannot. A bicycle is a system of transport to enable travel from A to B. It has within it a braking system, a gear system, and so on. None of these systems enable, on their own, travel from A to B.
Epistemology	The study of how we know what we know.
Expert System	A computer program developed to simulate human decisions in a specific field or fields. A branch of artificial intelligence.
Explicit Knowledge	Knowledge that can be shared by way of discussion or by writing it down and putting it into documents, manuals or databases.
Externalization	The transformation of tacit knowledge into new explicit knowledge.
Hard Systems Thinking	This takes the approach of Reductionism and assumes that there are well-defined agreed technical problems that can be solved with a single optimal solution, using a rigid scientific approach is the way to solve problems. Compare with Soft Systems Thinking and Critical Systems Thinking.
Holism	Holism is the concept of a system whole being greater than the sum of is parts. It encompasses the notion of Emergent Properties. Holism is sometimes viewed as the antithesis of Reductionism.
Information	Data that has been arranged into meaningful patterns and thus has a recognizable shape.
Information Processing	Sciences concerned with gathering, manipulating, storing, retrieving and classifying recorded information.
Information Quality	Discerning which information sources are more useful and accurate than others.
Information Resource	Any entity, electronic or otherwise, capable of conveying or supporting intelligence or knowledge.
Information Systems	The general term for computer systems in an organization that provides information about its business operations.

Intellectual Capital	Knowledge (that can be converted into value or profit) and skills that lead to a competitive edge in the marketplace.
Intelligence Continuum	The systematic process of diagnosing any output from a system using the key tools, techniques, tactics and technologies of the knowledge economy, i.e. data mining , KM and business intelligence, to ensure that at all times the future state builds on the current state.
Internalization	The transformation of explicit knowledge into new tacit knowledge.
IT Management	The manner or practice of managing IT, specifically regarding handling, supervision or control.
IT Strategy	An elaborate and systematic IT plan of action.
Knowledge Architecture	The blueprints for identifying where subjective and objective knowledge and/or tacit and explicit knowledge reside in an organization.
Knowledge Assets	Knowledge regarding markets, products, technologies and organizations, owned by an entity allowing it to generate profits and add value.
Knowledge Capture	The process of acquiring and storing information, ideas and relationship links in the people, processes and technology within an organization.
Knowledge Creation	The creation of new ideas and thoughts.
Knowledge Delivery	The act of conveying knowledge.
Knowledge Infrastructure	The design of the socio-technical requirements for ensuring appropriate KM, i.e. the design of the necessary people and technology requirements for facilitating KM in a specific organization.
Knowledge Management	The creation and subsequent management of an environment which encourages knowledge to be created, shared, learnt, enhanced, organized and utilized for the benefit of the organization and its customers.
Knowledge Nugget	A small but important piece of knowledge.
Knowledge Retention	Keeping ideas and thoughts within an organization.
Knowledge Sharing	Mechanisms to communicate and disseminate knowledge throughout an organization.
Knowledge Spiral	The transformation of one type of knowledge to another.
Knowledge-Based Systems	Computer programs designed to simulate the problem-solving behavior of human experts within very narrow domains or scientific disciplines—this discipline is a sub-set of Artificial Intelligence.

Learning Organization	An organization that views its success in the future as being based on continuous learning and adaptive behavior.
MIS	Information systems designed for structured flow of information and integration by business functions and generating reports from a database.
Narrative	A telling of some true or fictitious event or connected sequence of events.
Objective Perspective of Knowledge	Following the Lokean/Leibnitzian forms of inquiry , such knowledge facilitates greater effectiveness and efficiency.
Ontology	The study of what exists; the categorization of things. Often used inter-changeably with Taxonomy.
OODA Loop	See Boyd's Loop.
Organizational Culture	Comprises the specific collection of values, norms, attitudes, experiences and beliefs that are shared by people and groups in an organization.
Organizational Learning	The ability of an organization to gain knowledge from experience through experimentation, observation, analysis and a willingness to examine both successes and failures, and to then use that knowledge to do things differently.
Procedural Knowledge	Knowing rules, methods and documented organizational norms. Procedures— "know what," "know where," "know who," "know how." Compare with Declarative Knowledge.
Reductionism	Reductionism is about the view that a system can be explained by science or an approach to understanding a complex system by consideration of its component parts. Reductionism is sometimes seen as the antithesis of Holism.
Socialization	The transformation of tacit knowledge into new tacit knowledge.
Social Capital	Represents the degree of social cohesion that exists in communities. It refers to the processes between people which establish networks, norms, and social trust, and facilitate co-ordination and co-operation for mutual benefit.
Social Network	A social structure comprised of nodes, individuals or organizations that are tied together by one or more types of interdependency.
Social Networking Site	An online community of people who share interests and activities.
Soft Systems Thinking	Soft systems thinking is a holistic approach that aims at understanding problem situations and agreeing what problems exist, with a view to resolving the problem situation. Organizations are viewed as complex social systems in which resolution, as opposed to solution, is sought by debate. Compare with Critical Systems Thinking and Hard Systems Thinking.
Storytelling	Use of anecdotal examples to illustrate a point and effectively transfer knowledge.

Strategy   Strategy is about long-term planning to achieve competitive advantage.

Subjective   Following the Hegalian/Kantian schools of inquiry, such knowledge facilitates
Perspective of   sense making and innovation.
Knowledge

System   A set of bounded activities, entities and their relationships that together
                        comprise purposeful activity that has at least one Emergent Property not
                        exhibited by the individual components within the set.

Systems Thinking   The study and organization of parts and their dynamic relationships, that
                        comprise a whole, rather than the study of static organizational parts.

Tacit Knowledge   The knowledge or know-how that people carry in their heads. Compared with
                        explicit knowledge, tacit knowledge is more difficult to articulate or write
                        down and so it tends to be shared between people through discussion, stories
                        and personal interactions.

Taxonomy   The categorization of things. Often used inter-changeably with Ontology
                        (meaning 2).

Notes

1   This case exercise was prepared by Dr Wickramasinghe with the assistance of her students Richard Morrow, Devaraj Ramsamy, Vernell Robinson and David Rogers to facilitate class discussion rather than illustrate effective or ineffective management practices. Only publicly available information has been used to write this case and it does not reflect any opinions of employees at this organization.

2   This case was prepared by Dr Nilmini Wickramasinghe with the assistance of Manuel Gayle as the basis for class discussion rather than to illustrate either effective or ineffective handling of an administrative situation. Only publicly available documents were used and no employee perspectives are reflected in this material.

3   This case was prepared by Dr Nilmini Wickramasinghe with the assistance of her students Kevin Grisez and Siobhan Sudberry as the basis for class discussion rather than to illustrate either effective or ineffective handling of an administrative situation. Only publicly available material was used and no employee opinions are reflected in this material.

4   This case was prepared by Daren Thompson as the basis for a class assignment rather than to illustrate either effective or ineffective handling of an administrative situation. Company names have been suitably anonymized.

5   This case was prepared by Dr Nilmini Wickramasnghe with the assistance of her students Monica Louie, Daniel Milosevic and Shad Sungren as the basis for class discussion rather to illustrate either effective or ineffective handling of an administrative situation. Only publicly available information was used and no employees opinions are reflected.

6   Source 1996 Consulting News published by Kennedy Information.

7   Keynote address by Microsoft at the 22nd Bled e-conference Bled Slovenia, June 15–18, 2008.

8   This case was prepared by Dr Nilmini Wickramasinghe for the purposes of class discussion only from publicly available documents. It is not intend to reflect effective or ineffective management use and in no way represents any thoughts or opinions of individuals at the company. All names have been changed.

Index

48037188R00089

Made in the USA
Middletown, DE
08 September 2017